131

THE CHRISTIAN KIDS ALMANAC

By ROBERT G. FLOOD

Illustrated By
Britt Taylor Collins

Chariot Books

Special thanks go to artist Kurt Mitchell, for the use of his illustration on page 103, and to photographer David Singer, for the use of his photos on pages 111 and 180.

Chariot Books is an imprint of David C. Cook Publishing

David C. Cook Publishing Co., Elgin, Illinois 60120
David C. Cook Publishing Co., Weston, Ontario

THE CHRISTIAN KIDS ALMANAC
Text © 1983 by Robert G. Flood
Illustrations © 1983 by Britt Taylor Collins

First printing, 1983
Printed in the United States of America
89 88 87 86 85 84 83   5 4 3 2 1

ISBN 0-89191-715-2

Library of Congress Cataloging in Publication Data

  Includes index.
  Summary: A collection of little-known facts and
unusual trivia on subjects related to Christianity and
Christian life.
   1. Christian biography—United States—Juvenile
literature. 2. Christianity—United States—Juvenile
literature. [1. Christianity—Miscellanea.
2. Christian life—Miscellanea. 3. Curiosities and Wonders] I. Title.
BR569.F57   1983   209'.73   83-5307
ISBN 0-89191-715-2

To my west coast nephew, Scott Regier,
and cousin, Tyler Francis,
and their millions of associates
in America's Christian and public schools

Did You Know ... ?

Did you know that a contraption called the Ezekiel Airship, built by a minister, may have flown before the Wright brothers' airplane did?

That in a major American city, Christian teens run their own tv station?

That a basketball team made up entirely of Christians defeated the Soviet Union team in a tournament in France?

That a man in Alaska puts Christian messages in bottles each year and throws them into the sea—by the hundreds?

These tidbits and many others make up *The Christian Kids Almanac.* An almanac is a book full of miscellaneous information. (The most famous one, *The Farmer's Almanac,* also talks a lot about the weather, and a new one comes out every year.)

The miscellaneous information in this book all has something to do with Christianity, both today and in the past, both in America and across the seas.

In these pages you and your family can read about Christian astronauts, jungle pilots, and the basketball player who turned down a $1 million pro offer to play instead for a Christian team.

You can join briefly the man who walked across America, two brothers who ran across the continent, and the cyclists who each summer bike across. Read the stories behind the Archie comics, Kentucky Fried Chicken, and the search for Noah's ark.

Meet also early Americans like Noah Webster, John Witherspoon, and George Washington Carver. Explore the frontier with circuit riders and pioneer missionaries.

Read about the Christian patriot who wrote "The Star-Spangled Banner," satellites that beam the gospel, and the incredible hoax of the Piltdown Man. In all, you and your family will find more than two hundred captivating entries.

The information in this book comes in bits and pieces, and in alphabetical order. So you can read it any way you want. You can start with the letter *A* or the letter *Z.* You can read one entry and put the book aside for later. Or you can read pages and pages!

Whatever you do, we hope you have fun—and at the same time, that you will learn a lot about what God has done for his children.

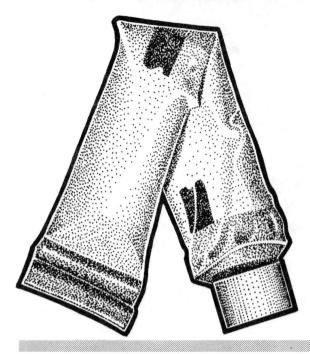

African Safari Artist

When Philip Lasz heads out on safari into the African wilderness, he looks hard for elephants, tigers, giraffes, and other wildlife. That's because he's a wildlife painter—one of the best in the world.

But how do you get close enough to draw wild animals? And how do you get a lion or cheetah or zebra to stand still long enough for you to paint his portrait?

Elephants stampede beneath Mt. Kilimanjaro.

Of course, you don't.

Instead of a rifle, Phil Lasz goes armed with a camera and a telephoto lens. It takes him some patience and waiting, because most animals won't stop and say "cheese." But eventually he gets the right shot. Back in his studio, he can paint the picture at leisure from a color slide.

Phil Lasz, also a missionary to Kenya, East Africa (his painting is a sideline), says he went on his first safari at the age of two months! He was a little too young, however, to remember it. You see, his parents were also missionaries to Africa.

Lasz was born and raised in what used to be called the Congo, and is now Zaire. So from his earliest childhood, he grew up around Africa's wildlife. When he paints these animals, he knows what he is doing. His paintings have won numerous awards and he has exhibited in New York, London, and Nairobi. He gives half of the profits from his art to the Lord's work.

SEND FOR: Animal Posters

You can purchase colorful 12-by-18-inch prints of the baby animal paintings you see at the top of the next page. Lasz did these caricatures especially for kids, trying to paint each with its own personality. Usually they sell for $3.50 each, but the Philip Lasz Gallery is giving readers of *The Christian Kids Almanac* a special price of only $2.00 apiece. Or you can buy the whole set of six for just $10.00.

Each painting is on heavy, canvas-textured paper. These are real award winners, and when you hang them up in your room, you'll love them! Write Philip Lasz Gallery, P.O. Box 6287, Rockford, Illinois 61125—and tell them *The Christian Kids Almanac* sent you! If you're ordering individual prints, identify which ones you want by giving the order numbers shown at left.

Our thanks to Max Anderson, Philip Lasz's agent in the United States, who arranged this special price.

Mr. Lasz paints in oils and acrylics, then reproduces the works as lithographs.

Air Force Style

The dramatic spires of the Air Force Academy Cadet Chapel sweep a towering 150 feet up into the Colorado Springs sky. This unusual chapel, which is visible for miles, is made of aluminum, glass, and steel.

Its airplane motif is also unique. Pews in the Protestant nave, on the upper level, are sculptured so that the end of each pew resembles a blade of an airplane propeller. And the back of each pew is capped by a strip of aluminum similar to the one on the leading edge of an aircraft wing!

This "all-faith house of worship" seats 1800 people.

Photo courtesy of USAF Academy

Amy

"Amy who?"

In case you have to ask that question, we're talking about singer Amy Grant. She is the top young female soloist on the Christian concert circuit, as far as many are concerned. Her record *Age to Age* has broken all sales records in the Christian recording industry.

Amy wasn't always a dedicated Christian. Even in the third grade, she says, she hadn't outgrown "temper tantrums." In the seventh grade, her church friends were being baptized, so she was baptized, too— just to go along with the crowd.

It was not until her freshman year in high school that she really saw what faith in Christ was all about. When one of the most popular guys in school invited her to his youth group, she went. She saw something different about the other kids she met there. Through their influence, Amy accepted Jesus Christ as her personal Savior that winter.

Though only fifteen at the time, she began to write songs about her new outlook on life. By the next August she had penned fifteen of them! Amy boldly asked the headmistress of the all-girls school she now attended if she could stage her first concert for the student body. Amy had taken piano lessons for some years, but now, in preparation for her first concert, she also learned to play the guitar.

She made a tape of the concert and sent it home to her mom and dad. They in turn passed it on to the leader of her youth group, who happened to be associated with Word Records in Waco, Texas. He was impressed. Not long afterwards—as a high school junior—Amy signed a contract with Word. Two years later she was singing in Billy Graham's Nashville crusade.

Amy sings about situations and feelings many Christian kids can identify with, as in the song "Giggle," written the week she graduated from high school:

> When I'm in a sticky situation,
> Sittin' in a class at school,
> Everybody's talkin' evolution,
> No one talks of you.
> My arm goes up.
> I don't wanna be too pushy.
> My arm, it feels like lead.
> But there's such a joy they're missin',
> Sayin' God is dead.

In the summer of 1982, Amy married Christian singer and songwriter Gary Chapman. They'd written and performed some songs together even before their wedding, so you can probably expect more teamwork from them in the future.

Archaeology: Kids at Work

Archaeologists—people who study objects from past cultures—sometimes unearth exciting things, such as mummies or buried treasure. Sometimes they work in pyramids or lost cities.

But most often, archaeologists do slow, painstaking work. Even little things such as

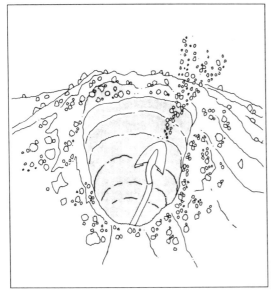

broken pieces of pottery, called shards, can give them important clues about life in the past—as a couple of junior archaeologists found out.

When Jonathan Borowski, aged thirteen, went with his archaeologist father on a two-week "dig" at Lahav, Israel, he thought he was going to be bored. He even took along a backpack full of books! But once on the site, he got involved after all. Day after day he worked in ankle-deep ash, digging and sifting, and then brushing off and washing any shards and bits of bone he found. Week after week he discovered nothing out of the ordinary.

Then one day he picked something out of the bucket of shards he was washing that felt different. The small, hard lump had figures of people in tall, pointed headgear etched into one side, and something that looked like the impression left by a rope or cord on the other. It turned out to be an ancient *bulla,* a clay seal used on an official document to keep it from being opened by the wrong person. Veteran archaeologists dated the seal at about 1500 B.C.!

Six-year-old Elizabeth Shanks had an even more unusual experience. While she and her family were looking for shards aboveground at a dig at Hazor, Israel, Elizabeth found a pottery handle with something carved in it. The carving turned out to be a picture of a pagan Syro-Hittite god from 1400 B.C., and helped archaeologists learn more about the Hittite people, who are mentioned in the Bible.

Elizabeth Shanks donated her find to the Hazor Archaeological Expedition, and received a letter from the head of the expedition, Yigael Yadin. Professor Yadin wrote, "I offer you my congratulations. . . . You spotted this handle at a place over which I and my fellow archaeologists walked many times without seeing it."

(For more reading about archaeology, see *Dead Sea Scrolls, Ebla,* and *Lost Ark.*)

FREE: Gift Brochure

Would you like to own a copy of the oldest board game in the world? Buy a set of historic coins? Fit pottery shards and fragments together into a replica of an ancient pot, just as an archaeologist would? Then you might be interested in the unusual books and products sold in the Biblical Archaeology Society gift brochure.

For a free copy of the catalog, send your request (along with your address) to: Biblical Archaeology Society, 3111 Rittenhouse Street NW, Washington, District of Columbia 20015.

Archie

Archie Comics are everywhere. You know Archie: a likable, freckle-faced teen who means well, but has a few weaknesses, just like we all do.

What you may not know is that Archie has been around for more than thirty years. That's how long ago cartoonist Bob Montana created him. But Archie, like many comic strip characters, has never aged.

Still he has changed. A few years ago, something tremendous happened to Archie. He became a Christian!

The story is told in the comic book, *Archie's Clean Slate*. But how did it really happen? To understand it all, you will have to meet another man, Al Hartley, the son of the author of the famed Taft-Hartley Act.

Even before Al Hartley was a teenager, he was drawing cartoons. As far back as he can remember, he had always wanted to be an artist. So after a stint as a military pilot,

Al plunged into the world of commercial art—every phase of it.

"Success was my goal," he says, "but it never occurred to me that success starts on the inside. I really wanted to make a bundle overnight."

He invested the money he made from his art in the stock market, and at one point even had a stock ticker installed in the studio of his home—a private wire from the floor of the New York Stock Exchange.

Later he became a cartoonist, producing comic books. His story strategy was to put the characters he drew into impossible situations.

"That was the name of the game," he says. "Lead the hero down a blind alley, tighten the web of circumstances that spelled curtains for him, and then—zip! With a flick of the pen, bring him out on top. It was easy! I did it every day!"

Al Hartley could make his comic-strip characters do what he wanted, but he couldn't handle the turmoil in his own life. Then some friends invited him to a prayer

PUT ME *DOWN !!!...*

meeting, and Al Hartley turned his life over to the Lord—lock, stock, and drawing board!

Soon afterward, out of the blue, the editor of Archie Comics phoned and asked Hartley to take over the drawing of "the king of the comics." (Bob Montana had retired.)

It was an unbelievable opportunity. At that time Archie already appeared in over 850 newspapers around the world. He had his own tv show on CBS each week. Every year over sixty million comic books were sold featuring Archie and his friends.

Al Hartley wanted to make Archie a Christian. In his first attempt to include Christ in a Christmas issue, the editor vetoed the story. But eventually the editor told him he no longer had to submit plots and scripts for approval before doing his illustrations. He could just mail in his finished cartoons.

Hartley knew Archie's potential for influencing kids spiritually was enormous. Soon after that, Al Hartley successfully made Archie a Christian.

(For a look at cartoons kids are producing today, see *Cartoons.*)

SEND FOR: Archie Comic Books

The Archie Comics, and other Spire Comics, can usually be found at your local Christian bookstore. If there is no such bookstore in your area, you may order them at sixty-nine cents each, plus fifteen cents postage and handling from: Spire Comics, Fleming H. Revell Company, P.O. Box 150, Old Tappan, New Jersey 07675. (Minimum mail order is four copies, which would cost $3.36.)

Titles in the Archie series include: *Archie Gets a Job, Archie's Clean Slate, Archie's Love Scene, Archie's One Way, Archie's Parables, Archie's Something Else, Archie's Sonshine, Archie's World,* and *Archie's Family Album.* Your order must indicate the titles you want.

Illustration by Al Hartley from Archie and Big Ethel, *used by permission*

Art Contests

Who are the Michelangelos of tomorrow? No one knows, but some kids are certainly practicing their artwork. The scene on this page was drawn by David Earl, age fourteen, of South Wales, Australia; it won him a grand prize award in *Young Ambassador* magazine's annual contest.

The *Young Ambassador* contest is open to junior high and high school students (no older than nineteen). In addition to the art category, the contest also includes photography, puzzles, and writing: fiction, nonfiction, personal experience, devotional, fictionalized biblical story, and poetry. (See separate entries under *Photography, Puzzles, Poetry,* and *Writing.*)

The contest deadline is usually March 15, with winners announced in August. Winners are notified by mail, and their material will be purchased for use in YA at rates ranging from $5 to $100.

Before you enter, be sure to write for the contest rules: *Young Ambassador,* Box 82808, Lincoln, Nebraska 68501.

Young teen art is also sometimes purchased for use in many Sunday school papers, such as *Sprint* (David C. Cook Publishing, 850 North Grove, Elgin, Illinois 60120) and *Teen Power* (Scripture Press, 1825 College Avenue, Wheaton, Illinois 60187). You could also write to your denomination's Sunday school headquarters and ask about submitting work there.

An Australian 14-year-old won a prize for this ink drawing of his homeland.

Astronaut's Viewpoint

"I saw no God nor angels," reported Soviet cosmonaut Gherman Titov after he returned from his pioneer orbit of our world in 1961.

But when *Apollo 15* astronaut James Irwin stood on the moon in 1971 and looked back at the planet Earth hanging in space, his response was just the opposite. He was overwhelmed by God's tremendous love. And there he also decided that, once back on Earth, he would tell others about Jesus.

The astronaut kept that promise. Today he travels around the country and abroad, speaking to many young people and even heads of state about space and the gospel. Sometimes other Christian astronauts join him.

The mobile space museum he developed

for the bicentennial year, "From Outer Space to Inner Space," emphasizes both America's achievements in space and the spiritual values upon which America was founded. This exhibit is now on permanent display at the NORAD Visitors Center of Peterson Air Force Base near Colorado Springs.

Displays inside the museum, constructed on a long semitrailer, include many color photos taken on *Apollo 15,* films of lunar exploration, Colonel Irwin's space suit, lunar tools, a moon rock, a space food exhibit, and an American flag of the type planted on the moon.

One of the lunar exploration films replays Colonel Irwin's quote from the Psalms while on the surface of the moon. Other panels quote from Genesis about the creation of the sun and the moon.

(For other articles on space, see *Bible in Space, Moon,* and *Space Shuttle.* For another article on James Irwin, see *Noah's Ark.*)

SEND FOR: Space Flight Patch

You may not ever get to the moon (or you just might, too), but you can still decorate your jacket, jeans, or schoolbag with an official NASA Space Flight Patch. The patch has the letters *NASA* and stars embroidered in white on a blue background, with red for a nice accent.

Send one dollar plus twenty cents for postage and handling to: Hayden Planetarium Museum Shop, Eighty-first St. and Central Park West, New York, New York 10024 (New York state residents add eight cents tax).

Atheist No More

The headline "Boy, 14, Balks at Bible Reading" accompanied a news story and the photo you see here on the front of the *Baltimore Sun* in 1960. The boy was William Murray, son of atheist Madalyn Murray O'Hair.

Madalyn Murray, an admirer of communism, had just tried unsuccessfully to defect with her two sons to the Soviet Union. Back in America to enroll son "Billy" late at a Baltimore junior high, she passed a classroom and observed the kids standing by their desks, heads bowed, as they recited the Lord's Prayer. Furious, she stormed to the principal's office, determined from that point on to stop this violation of her religious rights as an atheist.

Billy went along with his mother's protest—at the cost of much ridicule by classmates. He helped her staple, fold, and mail her monthly atheist newsletter. Madalyn Murray and her son filed a lawsuit against the school system, which eventually went all the way to the Supreme Court.

On June 17, 1963, in an historic decision, the Supreme Court ruled 8-1 in the Murrays' favor. School-sponsored prayer and Bible reading were expelled from the classroom. In fear of lawsuits, many other schools went even further, and banned before-school and after-school Bible clubs.

For years William Murray continued to work for atheistic causes. His personal life was a mess. But on January 24, 1980, he was awakened in the middle of the night by a terribly disturbing dream. The dream prompted him to climb out of bed and search out a Bible at an all-night discount store. Back in his apartment, he eagerly devoured the Gospel of Luke. That night he invited Jesus into his life.

The change in his life was dramatic. Where he had once seethed with hate, he felt love. A few weeks later he wrote a letter to the *Baltimore Sun*. It read in part:

". . . I would like to apologize to the people of the City of Baltimore for whatever part I played in the removal of Bible reading and praying from the public schools of that city. . . . Being raised as an atheist in the home of Madalyn O'Hair, I was not aware of faith or even the existence of God. As I now look back over 33 years of life wasted without faith in God, I pray only that I can, with His help, right some of the wrong and evil I have caused. . . ."

Billy's atheistic beliefs put him in the news.

Photo from the Baltimore Sunpapers

The letter of apology created a storm of publicity, and articles soon appeared in *Time* and *People* magazines. Since then William Murray has formed a Christian foundation and crisscrossed the country warning people of the dangers of atheism. In April 1982, he and several others delivered to the White House petitions bearing the signatures of one million Americans who want freedom for voluntary prayer in public schools.

William Murray, by the way, continues to pray daily for his mother.

Athletes in Action

Athletes in Action, the sports ministry of Campus Crusade for Christ, has been making a growing impact across the United States and around the world.

AIA recruits Christian athletes from the nation's colleges and universities, and sends them out in squads to compete and to witness for Christ. Its most prominent sport has been basketball (see *Basketball*), but AIA is fielding some remarkable teams in other sports as well.

Its track team, for instance, has grown most quickly, and is now the largest of all the AIA competing teams. It hopes to have ten members on the 1984 United States Olympic team, and AIA hopes to be named "official chaplains of the Olympics."

The AIA gymnastics center in southern California featured twenty All-Americans in one of its recent exhibitions. (The center is open to youths ranging from three years old to nineteen.)

In the summer of 1982, AIA sent its wrestling team to Latin America, its men's and women's basketball teams to the Orient, and one of its two baseball teams to Sweden. Everywhere they go, the athletes testify and sing of Jesus, speak in churches, hold sports clinics, and talk to individuals about their personal faith. You can read about the teams' activities in the organization's magazine (see *Magazines*).

AIA summer camps, open to teenagers, are also growing. In 1982 there were wrestling camps in six states, a running camp in Colorado, and girls' basketball and volleyball camps in southern California.

For information about these summer camps, you may write to: Athletes in Action Camps, 17102 Newhope Street, Fountain Valley, California 92708.

Awana

What does the word *Awana* mean?

First of all, it means a fast-paced club for kids, featuring games, Bible memory work, singing, skill handbooks, uniforms, and more. With programs geared to every age level of boys and girls from preschool to high school, Awana clubs meet weekly in churches throughout the country.

Second, *Awana* is a code word. The letters each stand for a word in a phrase that's the club motto, inspired by 2 Timothy 2:15—"Approved Workmen Are Not Ashamed."

For information about the clubs, write: Awana Youth Association, 3201 Tollview Drive, Rolling Meadows, Illinois 60008.

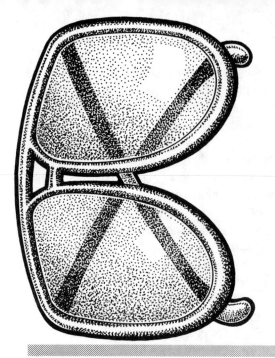

Balloons—and What?

On August 17, 1978, a Sunday school teacher—Maxie Anderson—and two other American men gently settled their silvery hot-air balloon into a wheat field in France. They stepped jubilantly out of their brightly colored gondola onto solid ground. The news spread quickly, and the world cheered.

The men had completed history's first transatlantic crossing in a balloon. They had drifted from the coast of Maine to France—more than three thousand miles— in just six days.

Since then Anderson and his friend Don Ida have made three attempts to circle the world, all daring but unsuccessful.

In February 1981, they launched a balloon from Egypt and drifted as far as India, where a leak kept them too low to cross the Himalayas.

In December 1981, the balloonists tried to start again from India, but got only thirty miles before the numbers painted on the balloon ate through the thin polyethylene and they were forced to land.

In November 1982, they lifted off into the cold sky from near Rapid City, South Dakota, but fourteen hours later their leaking craft had to land north of Toronto, Canada. A group of children in a school bus saw the huge balloon, named the *Jules Verne*, descend into a farm field.

Meanwhile, in the summer of 1982, a man in southern California pulled a balloon stunt not as professional as Anderson's, but certainly daring.

Larry Walters attached more than forty weather balloons to—would you believe it—his lawn chair! He took aboard oxygen tanks, jugs of water, a CB radio, a parachute—and a BB gun! Then he lifted off!

His strange rig soared into the skies, higher and higher, until he had reached sixteen thousand feet—higher than the altitude of California's Mount Whitney!

Two airline pilots spotted Walters and reported what they saw as a UFO.

Meanwhile, it was cold up there, and Walters had not brought along the proper clothing for the occasion. So he pulled out his BB gun and began to pop the weather balloons, one by one. Gradually he made his descent. He landed in some power lines, and had to jump the last five feet to the ground.

The Federal Aviation Authority didn't exactly like what Walters had done, not to mention the risk he had taken with his own life.

But how would they charge him?

There were no laws on the books about "flying lawn chairs"!

Baseball Chapels

On a typical Sunday morning before a game, many of today's major league baseball players can be found holding church in their clubhouses!

The chapel idea first took hold in the pro football ranks, then in pro baseball. Detroit sportswriter Watson Spoelstra initiated Baseball Chapel back in 1972, at the request of a handful of players who had been struggling to get their teammates out to church services. A ballplayer's tight Sunday time schedule, road trips, and the pressure for autographs when he attends church often work against a regular church life.

Why not, the Christian players suggested, attempt to bring such services directly to the players in the locker room and clubhouse?

The program began with only two clubs: the Minnesota Twins and the Chicago Cubs. Then Spoelstra approached baseball commissioner Bowie Kuhn, who gave his OK for a full-scale program, with Spoelstra as coordinator. The chapel has mushroomed far beyond anyone's expectations, now serving all twenty-six major league teams.

Players agree that the chapel program meets a need. "It is a pause for us to rest and reflect where we are and where we're going," said Dodger Ken McMullen. Harmon Killebrew, former Detroit Tiger player, added, "It reminds us that baseball isn't the number one thing in life."

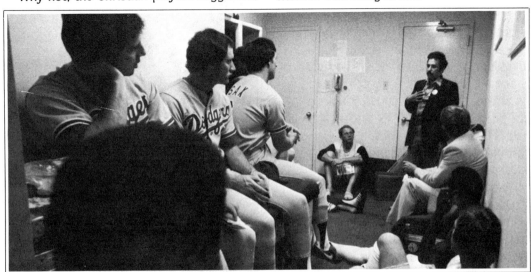

Baseball Coach

Al Worthington is the baseball coach for the fast-growing Liberty Baptist College of Lynchburg, Virginia. His team is already a major contender against NCAA Division One schools.

Before coaching, Al Worthington was a seasoned pitcher in the American League. He turned in a fine record with the Minnesota Twins. In earlier years he also pitched for the Chicago White Sox.

Until the day he quit the team.

At that time the Chicago White Sox had been "stealing the signals" of the other team. That meant they had someone posted out in the bleachers with a pair of high-powered binoculars. If the catcher on the opposing team called for a fastball, for example, then the spotter could pick up the signal and quickly relay this intent to the White Sox batter by a predetermined signal from the bleacher position.

Al Worthington, a devout Christian, didn't think this was right. Others disagreed. After all, they argued, weren't some of the other teams doing it, too?

When Al Worthington stuck to his guns, he lost his position with the White Sox. But soon God opened even better doors for him with the Minnesota Twins.

Baseball Profiles

Tommy John
Pitcher, California Angels

Tommy John is only the seventh pitcher in the history of baseball to have a 20-win season with both the National and the American leagues (once with the Los Angeles Dodgers and once with the New York Yankees). In 1982 he posted another impressive year, and pitched the California Angels to victory in the second game of the American League play-offs.

But on July 17, 1974, when he severely tore a ligament in his left elbow, doctors told him his baseball career was over.

Tommy John did not accept that diagnosis as final. Instead, he undertook a rigorous program to rebuild his arm, against all odds. He and his wife, Sally, also prayed hard and trusted in the Lord.

His comeback was miraculous.

Then on August 13, 1981, tragedy again struck the pitcher's life.

Tommy and Sally John's three-year-old boy, Travis, fell from a third-story window onto his family's station wagon, and then onto the driveway. Critically injured, he lingered in a coma for days as Yankee fans and opponents alike prayed for the son of the New York pitching star.

Today, his dad says, little Travis is completely recovered. Again Tommy John and his wife saw tragedy turn to victory. And again God's mercy has given them a chance to let the nation see their faith in him.

Photo courtesy of California Angels

Lamar Johnson
First Baseman, Texas Rangers

If you have ever played team sports, you probably know firsthand what it feels like to sit on the bench while the coach puts in someone else.

Lamar Johnson of the Texas Rangers sat on the bench for much of his 1981 season with the Chicago White Sox. Johnson's contract was about to run out. The White Sox limited his playing time, it seems, because they didn't want to sign him on again and wanted to see what the team could do without him. Johnson sat frustrated at first, because he needed good statistics to land a good contract with another team when he became a free agent in 1982.

He might have sulked, but as a Christian he decided to make the best of it. In fact, he became the team's most vigorous cheer-leader. At the end of the season some of his teammates said they didn't know how he was able to handle it all year. But Johnson said he had simply turned the problem over to the Lord.

Photo courtesy of Texas Rangers

Gary Lavelle
Pitcher, San Francisco Giants

How would you handle hostile press coverage? Pitcher Gary Lavelle, who is looked upon as a sort of "chaplain" by his fellow San Francisco Giants, can tell you.

For several years, the San Francisco Bay area press criticized Lavelle and some of his born-again teammates for the fact that they had positive attitudes whether the team won or lost. The press interpreted this as apathy, and even went so far as to blame a Giant slump on "the Christians." Lavelle gently reminded the press that he had been just as much a Christian during his winning streaks as he had been in his pitching slumps.

Then in 1981 a New York writer quoted Lavelle as saying the Bay area was "spiritually oppressed." Lavelle was referring to problems with sin, but the article interpreted it as an attack upon Bay area people.

With the encouragement of fellow Christians on the team, Lavelle refused to sling any mud back. The sportswriter later wrote and told Lavelle that he admired the pitcher's restraint in the situation.

Baseball Profiles, continued

Andre Thornton
First Baseman, Cleveland Indians

Andre Thornton can tell you how important it is to be fully honest, especially if you are known as a Christian. In 1978, during a batting slump, Thornton was approached by a man who knew how to put cork in bats. The cork was used by other players, but it was illegal. Thornton already used a black bat, so the filling could be all the more easily disguised. Two such bats were made for him, and Andre soon hit two tremendous home runs.

It was a great feeling, but he felt guilty about it later. "What would happen," asked a friend, "if one of the bats cracked and the people saw *you* using cork?"

The previous year Thornton had hit twenty-eight home runs, placing fourth in league home runs and RBIs—without help from cork. That was also the year he had won the Roberto Clemente Award for humanitarianism in baseball and the Danny Thompson Memorial Award for "exemplary Christian spirit in baseball."

Thornton had the bats destroyed.

No one who knows Andre Thornton doubts that his Christian faith is real. On October 17, 1977, Thornton's wife and daughter were killed in a tragic auto accident. Thornton and his son Andy, now age ten, survived.

Cleveland Indians manager Jeff Torborg still remembers the funeral as "the most moving experience of my life." Thornton shared his faith at the funeral service and said he was sad on the outside, but at peace on the inside. He urged everyone in the audience to trust Christ that day before another one of them died.

Nearly two years after the auto accident, God gave Andre Thornton another wife— Gail Jones, daughter of Howard Jones, an associate evangelist with Billy Graham. The same day, in a double ceremony, Gail's sister Phyllis married Pat Kelly, Andre's fellow Cleveland Indians teammate and also a Christian! The two sisters, together with their major league husbands, hope to start a Christian camp and conference center to reach the kids of Cleveland's inner city.

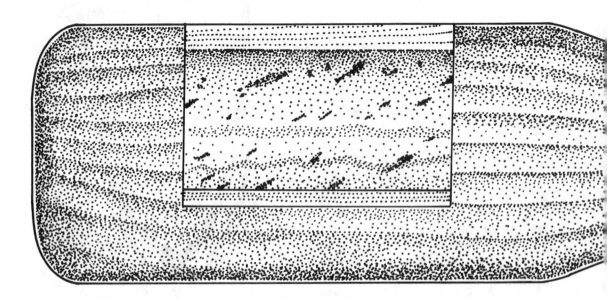

Baseball Sportscaster

If you live in Michigan, the voice of Ernie Harwell is probably familiar to you. Every year from April to October, he describes the play-by-play action of the Detroit Tigers. He has also handled the play-by-play commentary for two World Series, two All Star games, and every American League divisional play-off game since 1976.

Shortly after joining the Detroit Tigers in 1960, Ernie changed from a silent to a vocal Christian, thanks to a Billy Graham Easter service. "I thought it was ironic," he says, "that as a broadcaster, talking to thousands every day, I didn't have enough courage to stand up for Christ."

He regularly attends Baseball Chapel, along with nearly three-fourths of the Tigers players, and often speaks to groups about his faith in Jesus.

As a hobby, Ernie has also become a songwriter, with one song ("I Don't Know Any Better") recorded by B. J. Thomas. When Hank Aaron was moving in on Babe Ruth's home-run record, he wrote a song, popular at the time, called, "Move Over, Babe, Here Comes Henry"!

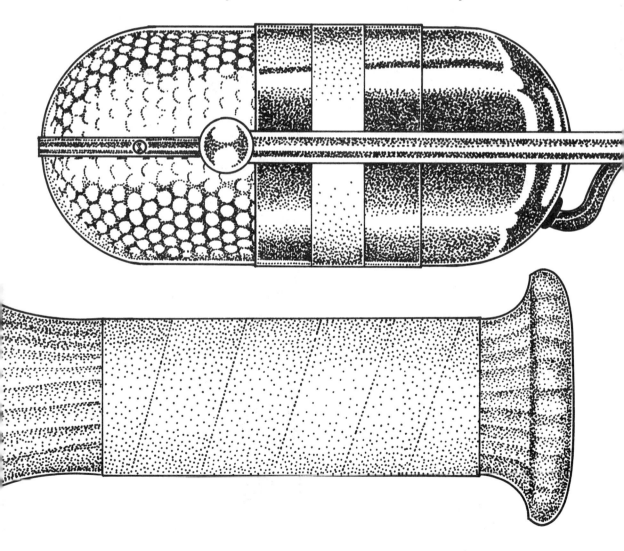

Basketball: Athletes in Action

The French crowd was on its feet sending chants of "USA! USA! USA!" reverberating throughout the arena.

This day was December 28, 1979. The United States, represented in the prestigious French Christmas Classic Basketball Tournament by the Athletes in Action (AIA) amateur squad, was, incredibly, holding on to a three-point lead over the awesome Soviet Union national team.

The Russian team, winner of the recent European Championships, had lost only two games in western Europe in the previous five years. Nobody in Paris' Coubertin Arena thought the lead would last, but halftime had come and gone. . .

With five minutes remaining, Brad Hoffman brought the ball downcourt for AIA. . . . Twisting and turning, he drove to the basket. He slipped, but maintained enough balance to flip the ball up with a twist off the backboard. A hard-earned basket, and two more points.

And then the Russians began to show why they perennially rank at the top of the amateur basketball world. They began to press the younger American team and stole the ball twice for easy lay-ups. . . . Suddenly the Russians trailed by just one point, 72-71. Less than a half minute remained.

Derrick Jackson stole the ball from Russian point guard Stanislav Eremin and began dribbling madly across the floor using up as much of the clock as possible. Fifteen seconds . . . fourteen . . . Jackson was fouled with four seconds left.

Jackson stepped to the free throw line for the first shot of a one-and-one.

For the first time that afternoon the crowd was silent as Jackson's shot arched toward the basket. So quiet that one could almost hear the swish of the net as the ball sailed through. The crowd roared.

The second shot was crucial, too. Jackson wiped his forehead with the back of his hand and took the ball from the referee. He bounced the ball three quick times, looked up and with barely a pause put the ball in the air. Perfect!

The Soviets got the ball downcourt as expected, but an errant shot fell short, harmlessly. Athletes in Action had won 74-71, an incredible upset!

The Russian coaches wondered

how they would explain to Moscow what had happened to them in the French Classic. They were having difficulty translating "Christian team" into Russian, and finally came up with something close, but not close enough. The Kremlin sports authorities had a hard time understanding why their team had lost to a "group of priests!" . . .

Can a basketball team whose players all know Jesus as their Savior really hold its own against the best teams in the world?

The Athletes in Action, a team formed in

1967 by Campus Crusade for Christ, have proved it can be done. (The above excerpt is from the first chapter of *More than a Game* by Joe Smalley, © 1981 by Campus Crusade for Christ.)

Athletes in Action never play a game without giving testimony to Jesus Christ during the halftime period. They are men who have each dedicated at least a year of their lives—often more—to Athletes in Action when they could be playing college or pro ball. One player, Ralph Drollinger, turned down a three-year NBA contract that would have netted him over a million dollars so he could stay on with AIA.

This unusual basketball team first went on the road in the fall of 1967. They pulled off a few upsets along the way (University of Southern California, Kansas State, Cincinnati, and Maryland). But they got their big break in 1977.

On January 20 of that year, the Athletes in Action shocked the sports world by beating the number one team in the nation at that time, trouncing the University of San Francisco, 104-85.

Winning is not the most important thing for the players of Athletes in Action. But the successes of 1977, and other upsets since then have helped them share the gospel all over the world.

AIA also has teams in other sports. (For information, see *Athletes in Action.*)

FREE: Basketball Booklet

Did you know that the first basketball game was played with peach baskets and a soccer ball? Well, it was. Unusual facts like this can be found in an interesting, twenty-three-page booklet, *Basketball Was Born Here.*

Send a business-sized, self-addressed, stamped envelope to: Basketball Hall of Fame, Box 175, Highland Station, Springfield, Massachusetts 01109.

Basketball Profiles

Julius Erving
Forward, Philadelphia 76ers

His name is Julius Erving, but they call him "Dr. J." For more than a decade he has played brilliant basketball, and since joining the Philadelphia 76ers in 1976, he has led them to three NBA finals. He and Kareem Abdul-Jabbar are the only active players that have been named to the all-time NBA All-Star team.

In 1979, however, Dr. J wasn't so sure of his future. He suffered a groin injury in the last game of the NBA play-offs against San Antonio. The 76ers lost the game and the play-offs, and Dr. J had to take much of the heat for the loss. "I was the team's leader," he says, "and when you have superstar status you're always expected to come through."

The injury was slow to heal, and this forced the popular player to slow down and think about the really important things of life.

In early summer of that same year Dr. J went to a family reunion. "Imagine three hundred of your relatives in the same room," he says, "at the same time—over a three-day weekend. I probably didn't know 280 of them, but they all knew me, so I became the common denominator.

"As I met new relatives and talked with them, we traced our history back to 1837 and discovered I'd had a strong Christian influence in my family almost from the beginning. One uncle in particular said he had always prayed for me and that possibly two generations before I was even born, one of my relatives had asked the Lord to lay a blessing on me."

Dr. J was so touched that he sought this uncle's counsel, and, he says, "I saw a lot of things start to fall into place." Shortly afterwards, Dr. J asked Jesus Christ into his life as Savior.

Dr. J says his life has not been the same since. His wife, Turquoise, has also asked Christ into her life, and the couple are growing together in their faith. Whatever the future holds for his career, says Dr. J, "we're going to glorify the Lord."

Paul Westphal
Guard, New York Knickerbockers

It's great to be a good athlete, and also one who wants to follow the Lord. But be careful how you link God with sports success.

That's the caution of Paul Westphal, shooting guard for the New York Knicks, who has been twice named to the NBA All-Stars team.

Westphal is a solid Christian, and has been since childhood. But "I would never make a free throw in a game," he says, "and then say, 'God helped me make that basket.' What would I say if I'd missed it? Would I blame God?"

Dr. J's life changed dramatically in 1979.

Photo courtesy of Philadelphia 76ers

In an interview with a Christian magazine, Westphal said, "I'm sure God works in athletic events. But his ways are hidden from us. Obviously he doesn't count how many Christians are on each team, and then let the team with the most Christians win."

Nor can a Christian demand a winning game, he says. "That would be like a kid who couldn't see over the dashboard telling his father where to drive. God knows what's best."

So how *does* Jesus make a difference?

Westphal is convinced that athletes who become Christians often *do* improve, because "the Lord helps them be more emotionally stable. God helped me to mature, and to learn how to control my emotions."

The most important thing a Christian athlete can do, believes Westphal, is be a good example.

Paul shoots over a New Jersey opponent.

Photo courtesy of New York Knicks

Basketball's Tallest Player?

When George Bell played for Biola University (formerly the Bible Institute of Los Angeles), he was believed to be "the tallest player in the history of American collegiate basketball," according to the *New York Times*.

His height: seven feet, eight inches!

George Bell also wears a size 26 shoe.

From Biola, Bell turned pro in 1982 and signed with the Harlem Wizards, managed by a former trick dribbler of the Harlem Globetrotters. There Bell had to learn the goofy plays and razzle-dazzle that make the Wizards' routine unique.

Surprisingly, Bell never played basketball in high school, and even at Biola was only the backup center! In the 1981-82 season Biola won thirty-nine straight games before losing to South Carolina-Spartanburg in the championship game of the National Association of Intercollegiate Athletics.

When Bell travels on the road with his team, he usually asks the hotel in which he's staying to put two beds together end-to-end.

The most common question people ask him is, "How's the weather up there?"

George rises above his 6'3" and 5'4" teammates.

Photo courtesy of Harlem Wizards

Bees

"I'm gonna let the bumblebee be," says the lyrics of an old song. And that's not a bad idea. We all know that bees don't exactly make the best pets.

But the ways of the bee can be fascinating, and the Moody Institute of Science (see *Science Films*) has produced one of the most remarkable documentaries on bees you can find. It's called *City of the Bees.*

Here are some of the amazing facts this film reveals.

• A beehive has thousands of cells, but bees varnish each one of these after every use.

• Bees create their own air conditioning in the hive by distributing water through it and then fanning their wings.

• Bees have their own language. One bee can tell another bee everything about a good nectar source a mile or more away, through a complex, figure-eight dance.

The "waggle" of the dance indicates the sugar content of the food. The angle of the dance in relation to the sun conveys the direction of the food source. And the length of time spent on the waggle and the number of pulses of sound emitted in each buzz are a measure of the distance to the food source. With this information the bee knows just how much "fuel supply" to take to get there.

• The hexagon pattern of the honeycomb is the ideal and most efficient shape for multicell storage, combining maximum space with minimum building material. High-speed aircraft, in their construction, utilize the principle of the honeycomb.

• Though bees can live for years, they literally work themselves to death in five or six weeks!

With close-up photography, *City of the Bees* takes you right into the beehive, without fear. But the Moody Institute of Science cameramen will tell you it wasn't easy. They had to do a lot of retakes. Hot photographic lights kept melting the honeycomb!

SEND FOR: Bees Booklet

To learn more about the unusual world of the bees, send for the sixteen-page booklet, "City of the Bees," based on the film described above. Write to: Moody Institute of Science, 12000 E. Washington Boulevard, Whittier, California 90606. Enclose fifty cents with your request.

BBBb
bBBB
BbB...

VARNISH

Bible in Space

The postage stamp shown at right commemorates the flight of *Apollo 8* from December 21 to 27, 1968, which put the first men in orbit around the moon.

On Christmas Eve of that year, millions around the world watched the drama on their television sets. They listened in as astronaut Frank Borman talked with Mission Control in Houston. Then, as the space capsule orbited the moon and people of Earth got their first close-up look at the moon's surface, the astronauts read from the opening lines of Genesis:

William Anders started off: "In the beginning God created the heaven and the earth. And the earth was without form, and void; and darkness was upon the face of the deep. . . ."

James Lovell picked up at verse 5: "And God called the light Day, and the darkness he called Night. And the evening and the morning were the first day. . . ."

Borman closed with verse 9: "And God said, Let the waters under the heaven be gathered together unto one place, and let the dry land appear: and it was so. . . ."

Viewers everywhere were moved by the experience.

Atheist Madalyn Murray O'Hair, though, was furious.

It didn't make her any happier when the U.S. Postal Service announced its intention to inscribe the words, "In the beginning God . . ." on the *Apollo 8* stamp. She tried to stop it, but to no avail.

These four words say so much. God is behind all that we see in the universe. The more we discover, the greater we find our God to be.

(For information on Madalyn Murray O'Hair and her son, see *Atheist No More.* For more on man in space, see *Astronaut's Viewpoint, Moon Facts,* and *Space Shuttle.*)

SEND FOR: Moon Flight Button

If you would like an official button commemorating man's first orbit of the moon for your space collection, you can still obtain it. The button (3½ inches in diameter) pictures astronauts Borman, Lovell, and Anders and their *Apollo 8* mission of December 1968. Just send sixty-nine cents, plus twenty-five cents postage and handling, to: Hayden Planetarium Shop, Eighty-first Street and Central Park West, New York, New York 10024 (New York state residents add six cents tax).

SEND FOR: Apollo 8 Stamp

If you would like a brand-new, mint copy of the *Apollo 8* postage stamp, send fifty cents for postage and handling to: Robert Flood, *The Christian Kids Almanac,* Chariot Books, David C. Cook Publishing, 850 North Grove Avenue, Elgin, Illinois 60120.

Bible Memory Marathon

Believe it or not, in Evansville, Indiana, a group of kids memorized the entire New Testament and recited it in less than twenty-four hours!

That's right. The concept was simple. There are 260 chapters in the New Testament. It took just 260 willing teenagers, each memorizing and reciting one chapter apiece, to accomplish the task.

Some who recited chapters did not know Jesus as Savior beforehand, but made that discovery as a result of the Bible Memory Marathon. The audience was tremendously moved as well by the performance. Since then other churches have held similar marathons.

Bible "Smugglers"

In the United States, Bibles can be found in most homes, and in almost any bookstore. But that's not so in the Communist-dominated countries of the world. Behind the Iron Curtain, it is not at all unusual for a Christian to pay a month's wages for a Bible—if he can even find one!

Some years ago, a young Dutch boy who had recently become a Christian went to a world youth festival in Prague. There he saw thousands of young people determined to change the world with the teachings and writings of Karl Marx and V. I. Lenin. The boy knew the Bible could also transform the world by changing lives. But in Communist lands, he discovered, almost no one had a Bible, even though many people eagerly desired to read God's Word.

That's when this Dutch boy, who later became known as "Brother Andrew," decided he would start taking Bibles across the border into Communist lands himself. Each time he would pray that the border guards somehow would not see his Bibles, even though they were often in easy-to-find places—such as right on the seat alongside him! Time and time again God answered his prayers. The border guards would search the car ahead of him thoroughly, but wave Andrew on through with only a quick look.

Brother Andrew and his associates would later take Bibles into Communist lands around the world. In time he became known as "God's smuggler."

Christians who visit Russia and other Communist countries today often remember to take an extra Bible or two along with them, as a "gift for a friend" somewhere in these lands. This is not illegal—though the Bibles *could* be confiscated any-way—and it is a gift the recipient always highly values and treasures. Breaking the laws of the land by concealing Bibles or carrying large numbers of them is not advisable, however.

SEND FOR: Smuggler Comic Book

For information on how you may obtain the story of God's smuggler in comic book form, see instructions under *Archie.*

Big Trees

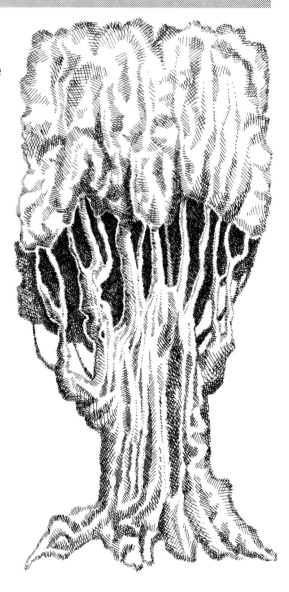

Where can you find the tallest tree in the world?

It's in northern California's Humboldt County—a coastal redwood that towers 362 feet into the sky. That's well beyond the length of a football field!

And the "fattest" tree? It's the General Grant tree in Sequoia National Park, with a circumference of more than 83 feet.

Northern California's two foremost Christian camp and conference grounds for kids and families are in or near the redwoods. The Mount Hermon conference grounds in the Santa Cruz Mountains are only two miles from Big Trees State Park, with trees almost as tall as the world's largest. Not far from Hume Lake Conference, in the Sierras, you will pass "General Grant."

The oldest known redwoods are about thirty-five hundred years old, which means they sprouted, perhaps, even before Moses led the Israelites out of Egypt.

Even these are not the oldest trees. Scientists believe the oldest living things on earth are some bristlecone pines in California's Inyo National Forest. They are estimated to be forty-six hundred years old!

(For more information about the camps, see *Camps.*)

Bill of Rights

Sounds like a musty document, doesn't it? Or a stuffy list of old-fashioned ideas. But the First Amendment of the Bill of Rights guarantees you and your parents the right to worship in church and practice your Christian faith.

Some students at Guilderland High School in New York State will tell you that this amendment cannot be taken for granted.

In early 1980, Jeanne Brandon, Jill George, Bill Smith, and a small group of their friends asked the principal if they could meet for prayer in a classroom before school. The students didn't expect any hassle, and that's where they were wrong.

The principal said, "No!" When these students and their parents took the case to court, declaring that their religious rights had been denied, a local court said "No!"

The next court in the legal process is the state court of appeals. Guess what? The New York State Court of Appeals also said, "No!" In fact, the court declared such practices on school property would be "too dangerous to permit." This case (*Brandon v. Guilderland School District*) was appealed to the highest court in our land, the United States Supreme Court. But the Court refused to review the decision. This led other courts in the nation to think that the Supreme Court agreed with the New York State courts.

Now many high school students in the United States are not allowed to meet on school property to pray and study the Bible—even on their own time there! Other student groups, however, may freely use school facilities.

A national group of Christian lawyers, the Christian Legal Society, based in Oak Park, Illinois, recently defended high school students in Lubbock, Texas, who were fighting a lower court ruling that denied their right to pray together on school grounds. The Supreme Court would not review this decision either. But the struggle goes on.

When you are tempted to think that the words of the First Amendment—"Congress shall make no law respecting an establishment of religion or *prohibiting the free exercise thereof*"—are not important to you or your friends, remember these Christian high school students. The vital sixteen words in the Bill of Rights are the basis for their right to meet together on school property for prayer and Bible reading.

Someday you, too, might have to defend your religious liberty. If so, the United States Constitution and the Bill of Rights will be your protectors and your guides.

Jeanne Brandon's prayer group went to court.

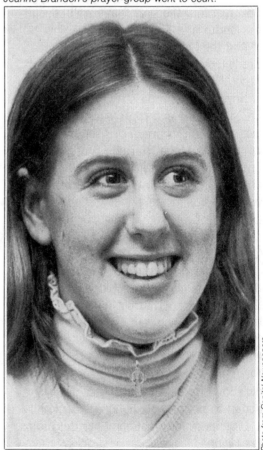

Photo from Capital Newspapers

Billy's Birthplace

The house in Charlotte, North Carolina, where Billy Graham was born has been replaced by a giant IBM building. But, very thoughtfully, IBM has mounted a marker showing people the precise site of the birth of this world-renowned evangelist.

Billy's home as a boy was a dairy farm, where he arose at 3:00 each morning to milk cows before going to school. Before he became a Christian at age seventeen, his ambition was to be a baseball player, and he did play a few semipro games for ten to fifteen dollars each.

After he turned his life over to Jesus, however, Billy suspected more and more that God might be calling him to be a preacher. To study toward that end, Billy enrolled in the Florida Bible Institute, and worked as a golf caddie and dishwasher to pay his way through!

If you've ever thought about being a preacher, it might comfort you to know that Billy's style did not "just come naturally." Wanting to practice preaching, but feeling rather shy about it, Billy regularly went to a cluster of trees alongside a river, stood on a cypress stump—and delivered his sermons to the unheeding Florida swamp.

Billy's preaching had him traveling even in 1948.

Book Club

Nowadays, much of what you read in the library seems to go against what your parents and the church have taught you is right. So it's nice to have books around that come at life from the Christian point of view.

Fortunately, many Christian books are being published today by companies that specialize in them, and they are being sold in special Christian bookstores. One of the largest conventions in the country now is the annual Christian Booksellers Association Convention, where booksellers come from all over the United States to see the publishers' newest products.

Hundreds of Christian books are available for kids, from comics and coloring books to mysteries and romances. You can get many of them at your local Christian bookstore. Or, if you go to a Christian school, your class can join the Christian School Book Club and order books through the mail. (If you're interested, have your teacher write for information to: Christian School Book Club, David C. Cook Publishing, 850 North Grove Avenue, Elgin, Illinois 60120.)

Books: Best-Sellers

When the *Bookstore Journal* in 1982 listed the top-selling Christian books for kids, many of the most popular (mentioned below) were for older kids like you. You'll probably be interested to note the kinds of books that won.

First place went to C. S. Lewis's Narnia Chronicles, seven fantasy books in which four British children are transported to another land, yet learn a lot about themselves and their own world (*The Lion, the Witch, and the Wardrobe; Prince Caspian; The Voyage of the Dawn Treader; The Silver Chair; The Horse and His Boy; The Magician's Nephew;* and *The Last Battle*).

Second place in number of sales went to some true tales about life in times past: the Grandma's Attic series, by Arleta Richardson (*In Grandma's Attic, More Stories from Grandma's Attic,* and *Still More Stories from Grandma's Attic*).

In ninth place came a rather humorous devotional by Lorraine Peterson, called *If God Loves Me, Why Can't I Get My Locker Open?* A cartoon-strip Bible, *The Picture Bible,* by Iva Hoth and Andre LeBlanc, came in tenth.

Another fantasy series came in a little further down the list: *The Princess and the Goblin, The Princess and Curdie, The Lost Princess,* and *The Golden Key,* by George MacDonald.

Other "top forty" sellers included *Pounding Hooves,* a horse story by Dorothy G. Johnston; the Elizabeth Gail mystery series by Hilda Stahl; *Dinosaurs: Those Terrible Lizards* by Duane Gish; *The Peanut Butter Hamster,* edited by Grace Anderson; and three devotionals: *Lord, I Have a Question* by Betty Skold; *Growing Up Isn't Easy, Lord* by Stephen Sorenson; and *Just a Minute, Lord* by Lois Johnson.

What was in the mystery trunk? The answer is in More Stories from Grandma's Attic, *by Arleta Richardson.*

Books: Most Expensive

What is the highest price ever paid for a printed book? The *Guinness World Book of Records* says it was $2.4 million. The product: one of the only twenty-one known complete copies of the Gutenberg Bible, printed in Mainz, West Germany, in 1454. It was bought by Texas University in a sale arranged in New York in June 1978.

Books You Write

Well, you don't exactly write them.

But when you read one of the Making Choices books from David C. Cook, you create your own plot line by choosing from different alternatives, and finally work your way to one of some thirty possible endings!

Every few pages in these books, the reader is presented with a choice. What do you want the character to do? Will you carry the strange man's box onto the plane for him or not? Do you explore the stream or the old mine? Should you call the police or try to catch the burglar yourself? These are just a few of the questions the books ask you. Some choices involve right and wrong, and some require common sense,

The choices you make could send you into space in The Cereal Box Adventures, *by Barbara Bartholomew.*

but some are just a toss-up.

One reader commented, "The nice thing about them is that you can read the book and make choices, then go back and make a different choice."

Though the Making Choices books are fun to read, they're tricky to write. Barbara Bartholomew, author of *The Cereal Box Adventures* and *Flight into the Unknown*, compared them to jigsaw puzzles. She and Donna Crow (author of *Professor Q's Mysterious Machine*) each made large charts to help them find their way through the maze of plots and endings. But it's fun once you get the knack of it, says Stephen Bly, who wrote *The President's Stuck in the Mud and Other Wild West Escapades*.

Barbara Bartholomew is convinced, however, that Making Choices books involve more than just fun. "In these books, things happen to you because of the choices you make," she says, and adds, "Isn't that the way real life is?"

A little kid helps you wear your dessert in one story line of the Making Choices book, The President's Stuck in the Mud, *by Stephen Bly.*

Book Writer

How many kids can say that they've helped write and publish a book? Not many.

But Karen McDonald of Haxtun, Colorado, is a bona fide writer. She coauthored a cookbook, and got it published.

It was her grandmother's suggestion. She invited ten-year-old Karen to help her write the cookbook. Together they had to decide their theme—one ingredient that would be common to all the recipes in the book.

They first considered peanut butter for their key ingredient, but then settled instead on cereal.

It was fun to eat the food they created.

"I was excited at first," says Karen, "but I did get tired of cooking after a while. We had about nine hundred recipes to test."

After all the recipes were tested, and the manuscript written, Karen and her grandmother, Betty McMichael, had to find a publisher. Several companies turned the book down before Christian Herald Books of Chappaqua, New York, accepted it.

Imagine their thrill when the book, *Cooking with Love and Cereal,* came off the press in 1981! Not only did Karen's name appear on the cover, but so did her picture.

What did it show her doing? Testing one of those nine hundred recipes, of course.

If you're interested in buying the book, send your inquiry to: Mrs. Betty McMichael, 3150 Eighteenth Street, Boulder, Colorado 80302.

Writing a cookbook means work, Karen learns—but at least the work tastes good!

Boone, Debby

If you're a typical kid, you know what it's like to hear your parents say no to something you really want to do. Singer Debby Boone also knows how that feels.

She was out of high school—no longer a "kid"—and wanted to launch her own singing career. (She had already recorded albums with her sisters.)

But her parents, Pat and Shirley Boone, said no. She wasn't ready for it, they said.

Though disappointed, Debby Boone looked around for other things to do. She and her boyfriend Gabriel Ferrer (who is now her husband) enrolled in a Bible school. Meanwhile, their pastor urged both of them to rise at 6:30 every morning and spend a half hour of quiet time with the Lord.

Debby knew it was a good thing to do, but how could she wake up at that time of the morning? She tried it, and before long each day seemed to go better. Debby grew in the Lord.

Then one day her mother walked into their kitchen in Beverly Hills, California, and announced that a music producer friend had just given her a cassette of a great new song. "He wants you to think about recording it," she said.

Could Debby really be hearing right? This suggestion came from her mother?

"No, I'm not kidding," her mother laughed. "Daddy's in the den. He'll play it for you. It's called 'You Light Up My Life.' "

Her dad also thought this was the right song, and finally the right time, for Debby to record on her own. Though written as a love song, the lyrics could also describe a person's love for the Lord.

The rest is history. A couple of years later, "You Light Up My Life" had sold over four million copies. It stayed at the top of the best-seller list longer than any previous song in twenty years!

Debby Boone says she is thankful now that her parents said no until they knew the time and the song was right. She is still looking for another hit song, but again it has to be the right one. "I'll hear a great song," she says, "but because just one line in the song disagrees with the stand I have taken morally, I can't sing it."

Debby and Gabriel (the son of actor Jose Ferrer and singer Rosemary Clooney) now have a son, Jordan Alexander Ferrer, and have made Jesus Christ the center of their home. Her biography, *Debby Boone—So Far,* has been published by Thomas Nelson, Inc.

If you're interested in reading about the pressures of Hollywood life, Debby's oldest sister, Cherry Boone O'Neill, has written a book for Continuum Publishing. Called *Starving for Attention,* it tells of God's help in her battle with anorexia nervosa, the "dieting disease" that affects thousands of young girls today.

Bottles at Sea

Have you ever put a message into a bottle and then tossed it into a river, or out into the sea?

Everett Bachelder of Nome, Alaska, has been sending messages in bottles for nearly thirty years. During the cold arctic winters, he and his wife stuff mayonnaise and peanut butter jars and ketchup bottles with gospel tracts—printed in as many as fifteen languages. Their eight children help.

Then in April, Everett Bachelder heads

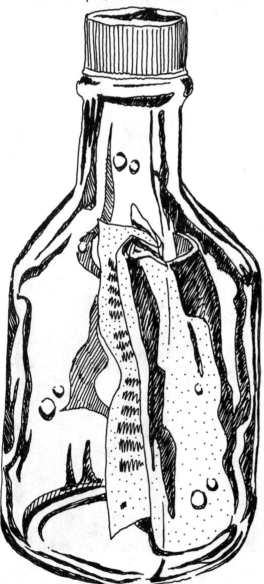

off by snowmobile or dogsled to the ice caves of the Bering Sea, where he drops them into the water. The May thaw sends the bottles out to sea. Sometimes tankers, freighters, or submarines help Bachelder with his massive bottle drops. He has launched more than thirty thousand bottles since it all began.

Where do the bottles go?

They have been found all over the world. Off the coast of Australia. Near Venezuela, New Guinea, Singapore.

They've crossed the Arctic Circle to be picked up in Iceland, Norway, Ireland, and along the west coast of Africa. "It takes at least ten years," says Bachelder, "for bottles to get through arctic ice packs, over to Norway, and down into the Atlantic Ocean."

And what do we know about people who find them?

On an ice floe north of the Seward Peninsula, an old Alaskan Eskimo sat deliberately freezing himself to death. He didn't want to be a bother to his children in his old age. Then he saw a bottle bobbing in some open water. In pain the old man crawled along the ice and grabbed it. The gospel message saved his life. The Eskimo wrote this note to Bachelder, who had put his name and address inside: "I read your tract and then I knew somebody loves me."

A crew member of a U.S. submarine patrolling in Mediterranean waters found a bottle and rushed it to the captain, who in turn wrote Bachelder in Nome. The captain told of his own Christian faith.

A young Buddhist was about to jump from the edge of a high cliff above the rocky Singapore coastline when he looked down and saw a bottle in the surf, ramming the rocks. *I'll wait until that bottle breaks before I jump,* he thought. But it refused to break. Distraught, he finally descended the cliff, retrieved the bottle, and read its message. Inside it told of Jesus' love and forgiveness. The Buddhist contacted a nearby mission station and accepted the Lord as his Savior.

"When we rest at night," says Bachelder, "we know the Lord is washing up another bottle on some distant shore."

By the way, it's not always tracts that travel in bottles. In early 1978, a young man in the Soviet Union heard a European Christian radio broadcast and decided he wanted a Bible of his own. He was afraid, however, to send his request through the mail. So he put a note in a bottle and addressed it to Earl Poysti, the man he had heard on the radio. The Soviet then threw it into the Baltic Sea and prayed.

Weeks later near Helsingborg, Sweden, a girl walking along the beach spotted the bottle. Inside she found the note, but she could not read it. A friend of hers guessed the lettering to be Russian, so they passed the note on to another friend who could translate it.

That person was Earl Poysti himself!

Promptly a friend of Poysti's was dispatched to deliver a Bible to the young Soviet. His prayer—and the message in the bottle—had been answered!

Boxcar Bunks

Have you ever wondered what it would be like to sleep in a railroad boxcar like a hobo? If you ever spend a week or two at Camp Willow Run in Littleton, North Carolina, you'll find out. The camp has turned old railroad boxcars into dormitories, all as part of the camp's unique railroad theme.

The dining hall is a depot!

Located on Lake Gaston, Camp Willow Run features sailing, canoeing, swimming, archery, and team sports—plus training in the Christian faith—for boys and girls ages eight to eleven. All aboard!

(For more about Christian camps, see *Camps*.)

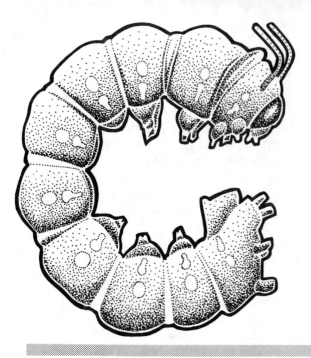

Camps

Is a Bible camp a part of your summer program? If so, you will probably go back to the same camp year after year. Once you make friends, that's where you want to be.

But maybe you have never been to camp, or your family is looking for other options. Tucked away in the hills and forests of America—often in some of the nation's most scenic spots—are literally hundreds of Christian camps and conferences.

Which state has the most? California does, with more than one hundred Christian camps. Michigan has nearly sixty.

If you want a complete reference, you can send for a 106-page *Guide to Christian Camps and Conference Centers,* describing more than seven hundred locations and where to write or call for complete information. The book sells for $6.95. Write Christian Camping International, P.O. Box 400, Somonauk, Illinois 60552.

Meanwhile, here are just a few of the many fine camps and conferences across the United States that *The Christian Kids Almanac* would recommend. (Others with a distinctly western style can be found under *Ranches.*)

● Camp of the Woods, Speculator, New York 12164. It has an excellent program of activities, speakers, and music for families, plus a terrific island camp for girls ages eight to sixteen, called Tapawingo. The densely forested island in the Adirondacks is rich in Indian lore.

● Deer Run/Brookwoods, Lake Winnipesaukee, Alton, New Hampshire 03809. Camp Deer Run is for girls ages eight to sixteen, Camp Brookwoods for boys the same age. Located on a quiet lake cove, the camps also sponsor trips to explore the nearby Mount Washington and the Swift River.

● Gull Lake Bible and Missionary Conference, Hickory Corners, Michigan 49060. Located on a lake near Battle Creek, Michigan, this camp's perfect for water sports and convenient for a tour of the nearby Kellogg's cereal factory. It's for families, but does provide youth activities.

● Honey Rock Camp, Three Lakes, Wisconsin 54562. Large forested acreage with lakes and rocky bluffs. Specializes in wilderness camping, including extended backpacking and canoe trips. Camp sessions are for two or four weeks.

● Camp Summer Life, Valdito, New Mexico 87579. Located in the beautiful Sangre de Cristo Mountains in northeastern New Mexico at 8,025 feet above sea level. Campers choose from a schedule of twenty-three activities, ranging from trout fishing and tennis to canoeing and overnight pack trips.

• Redwood Camp, Mount Hermon, California 95041. In the heart of the Santa Cruz mountains and redwoods. In addition to a whole list of outdoor and indoor sports, this camp even teaches you such skills as photography, dramatics, and guitar and ukulele playing. Junior campers may be surprised by a visit from Tom Sawyer and his gang; junior highers should watch out for "El Zero" during south-of-the-border fiesta time.

• Warm Beach Camps, Stanwood, Washington 98292. One hour from Seattle, with a dramatic view of both the Cascades and the Olympic Range. During summer,

the camp's "Chinook Village" hosts kids in the fourth to sixth grades, and the W-Bar-B Ranch handles those in grades seven to nine. Twelve horsemanship camps are scheduled May to September. For junior highers, there are week-long summer basketball camps, canoe camps, and trail camps.

These are just a handful of samples to whet your appetite. There are hundreds more.

SEND FOR: Camp Brochures

Free brochures of the camps listed above are available. Find out more about what they have to offer, the dates of their sessions, and their rates. The name of the camp, town, state, and zip code will be sufficient address. Also, tell them your age.

Carter's Hometown

While not everyone agreed with the politics of Jimmy Carter—as would be true of any president—all agree that he was not ashamed to express his Christian convictions.

President Carter taught a Sunday school class in Washington, D.C., urged his church to send out more missionaries, and at times even talked to world leaders about Jesus.

Plains, Georgia, the town where he grew up, still remains a tourist attraction. The Plains Depot is decorated with signs and bunting to let you know that it was once Jimmy Carter's campaign headquarters.

You can also see his birthplace, view some peanut warehouses, and scan the community where the former president grew up and reared his children. But you will have to be satisfied to wave at the Carter home from a distance, because of today's security precautions.

Of course, you never know just when the former president might decide to wander among the people in town and shake some hands.

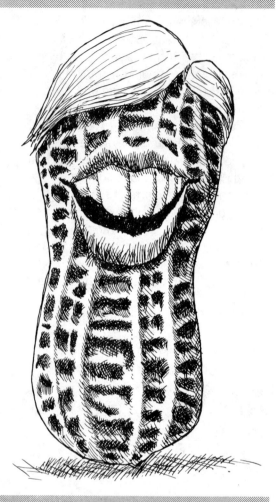

Cartoons

Everybody likes cartoons, because they're funny—yet they often manage to tell us something important at the same time. As a matter of fact, cartoons that make political and social comments are an important part of the editorial page in most newspapers today.

One well-known editorial cartoonist, the *Chicago Tribune's* Wayne Stayskal, is also a committed Christian, and many of his cartoons reflect this.

Stayskal, whose cartoons have been syndicated nationally since 1962, remembers mimicking comic strips in elementary

Wayne Stayskal began cartooning in grade school.

"It said another bad word!"

Dave Olsson, 15, drew this cartoon for Teen Power.

school. In junior high he did some cartoons for his church newspaper. Though raised in a Christian family, Wayne did not accept Christ personally until after high school, when he was in the Air Force. He went from the Air Force to art school, and soon after that to newspaper work. Besides drawing five editorial cartoons per week, Stayskal pens a syndicated sports cartoon called "Trim's Arena." He's had three books published: one of sports cartoons, called *Trim's Arena*, and two of editorial cartoons, *Hey, How Come They Get Steak and We Get Chicken?* and *It Said Another Bad Word.*

The other cartoons you see on this page are from *Sprint* and *Teen Power*, both young teen Sunday school papers. Perhaps some of these young humorists will go on to a career like Wayne Stayskal's. But even if they don't, it's fun to look on the light side of things!

If you'd like to enter *Teen Power's annual* cartoon contests, write for information to Cartoon Contest, *Teen Power*, Box 513, Glen Ellyn, Illinois 60137. You can also send cartoons to *Sprint*, 850 North Grove Avenue, Elgin, Illinois 60120.

Steve Patchett, 13, was published in Sprint.

Cattle for God

As you have traveled through farmlands, have you ever tried to count the cattle? It's not easy. Usually the car is going too fast for you to keep up a tally. Most of the cattle you see will go to market, and the rancher will keep whatever profit there may be.

But up in North Dakota and in some other parts of the country, there is a cow here, or a steer there, branded to indicate that its profits will go not to the farmer, but to world missions.

In California's San Joaquin Valley, for instance, the mark will probably be a missionary cross. If the rancher puts that brand on a cow, the profits from her calf each year will go to help support Christian missionaries, through a group called Missionary Supply Lines.

Near Bismarck, North Dakota, an organization called Steer, Inc. has involved numerous Christian ranchers in raising cattle for missions. And each year it holds a world missions roundup conference.

The idea fits perfectly with a verse from the Psalms: "For every beast of the forest is mine, and the cattle upon a thousand hills" (Psalm 50:10).

Chaplains Courageous

Military chaplains, or "pastors in uniform," minister in all the branches of our armed services. The postage stamp above commemorates the four heroic chaplains who perished on a sinking troop transport during World War II.

Off Greenland in February 1943, the enemy torpedoed the U.S.S. *Dorchester.* Many of those aboard feared the icy waters, but these chaplains calmed fears and persuaded sailors to go overboard, where there was a chance of rescue. (Many were later pulled to safety.)

They encouraged the men, prayed with them, helped them into lifeboats and life belts, and finally gave up their own life jackets.

As the ship's bow sank, men in the water and in lifeboats saw the four chaplains link arms and heard them raise their voices in prayer. They were still praying together on the deck when the ship made its final plunge.

SEND FOR: Four Chaplains Stamp

For a new, mint copy of the Four Chaplains stamp, printed about the story described above, send fifty cents (includes postage and handling) to: Robert Flood, *The Christian Kids Almanac,* David C. Cook Publishing, 850 North Grove Avenue, Elgin, Illinois 60120.

Chariots of Fire: Behind the Scenes

In 1982 the film *Chariots of Fire* seemingly came from out of nowhere to win three Academy Awards—including "Best Picture." A lot of people were surprised, since one of the film's main characters has a strong Christian message.

The true story centers around two young Britishers in the early 1920s, who both have Olympic potential. Cambridge University student Harold Abrahams, of Jewish descent, is determined to prove himself in the Olympics and bring credit to his race. The Scotsman Eric Liddell, an Edinburgh University student who plans to become a missionary, determines to run "for the glory of God."

Eventually both qualify for the 1924 Olympics in Paris, and both are scheduled to run in the 100-meter sprint. Then Liddell discovers that the qualifying heat for the 100-meter event is to be run on a Sunday. Because of his firm convictions about keeping the Sabbath holy, Liddell withdraws from the race.

The press reacts in shock. Britain had banked on Liddell to win a gold medal. Suddenly even his home country of Scotland begins to call him a traitor. But Liddell will not be swayed.

A team member then suggests that Liddell switch from the 100-meter race to the 400-meter, which is scheduled for a weekday. Liddell has never run the event, but he agrees.

On the Sunday of the 100-meter race, Abrahams wins the gold medal as Liddell cheers in the stands. Then comes the day for the 400-meter race. The opposition scoffs at Liddell's ability to run a longer race than he had trained for. The gun cracks, Liddell streaks off from his starting crouch, and the crowd cheers him to the finish line. He not only wins the event and a gold medal, but breaks a world record. If you saw the film, you already know all

Teammates cheer Liddell after he wins a gold medal.

Photo courtesy of Ladd Company/Warner Brothers

this. But you may not know these facts from behind the scenes:

• David Puttnam, the film's producer, got his idea for the film while lying ill, reading *The Official History of the Olympic Games.* Puttnam had previously produced the film *Midnight Express,* the story of an American's ordeal in a Turkish prison after smuggling drugs. Man at his worst. It would be a breath of fresh air, Puttnam thought, to produce a film showing man at his best. The result was *Chariots of Fire.*

• The scriptwriter altered some details of the story. In actual history, for instance, Liddell knew weeks ahead that the 100-meter heat would be run on a Sunday; he did not suddenly find it out en route to Paris. It was still an amazing feat, however, to run in a longer race

Liddell collapses after winning a race for Scotland.

than he had trained for, and win!

• Ian Charleson, who plays Eric Liddell, says he "read the Bible from beginning to end" in order to understand Liddell's strong Christian faith. "There is some incredible wisdom in the Bible," he says. Charleson also practiced hard to duplicate Liddell's unusual running style.

• *Chariots of Fire* ends after the Olympics. But Eric Liddell went on to serve as a missionary to China. In 1945 he died in a Japanese internment camp, but his life continues to inspire young people around the world who follow Jesus.

• *The Flying Scotsman,* released as a follow-up to *Chariots of Fire,* follows Liddell into China. It unfolds more completely the story of the Olympic runner who, right up to the end of his life, gave his all for the glory of God.

Photo courtesy of Ladd Company/Warner Brothers

Chimney Sweep

Look up on the rooftop. A figure dressed in black top hat and tails, with a brush over his shoulder. What is it? Who is it?

Meet Mike Sasnett, chimney sweep. His tools are a giant vacuum cleaner and an assortment of wire brushes.

But why such formal clothes?

Mike explains: "English and European chimney sweeps of yesteryear were among the very poorest of men. The sweeps received the used clothing of the morticians. Hence, the tradition and trademark."

The son of missionaries, Mike has had many unusual jobs. He has worked as an embalmer's apprentice, a Russian interpreter in the Navy, a private detective, a burglar-alarm installer, a land surveyor.

Every job he has held, says Mike, has helped to teach him "more of God's love and grace." Recently he donated three weeks of his time to the Wycliffe Bible Translators in Ecuador. There he and two others cut through thick jungle to do a land survey for the Quichua Indians.

Editor's Note: *The Christian Kids Almanac* has just learned that Mike Sasnett has a new job, diving for golf balls!

China's Surprise

A century ago, famed missionary Hudson Taylor pioneered Christ's work in the interior of mainland China. Later, many missionaries served in China—among them Eric Liddell. (See *Chariots of Fire.*)

But in 1949, the Communists, under revolutionary leader Mao Tse-tung, took control of the country, and expelled almost all the foreign missionaries. They used the churches for warehouses, museums, and other functions. They confiscated all Bibles. Many Chinese were killed for their faith. Christian groups had to meet in secret.

There were an estimated four million Christians in China at the time of the revolution. The Communists assumed these people would simply give up their faith—or eventually die off.

It did not happen.

Now that China has opened up to visitors again, the real story is getting out. There is evidence that there could be as many as twenty-five to fifty million Christians there. This is many times more than the estimated four million believers when the missionaries left!

Christian Service Brigade

One night each week, boys are going to hundreds of churches across America for the fun and learning of Christian Service Brigade.

If you are in grades three to six (ages eight to eleven), you can join the Stockade program. Stockades are divided by grades into smaller groups called posts, and each post of six boys has a trained adult leader. You would enjoy action-packed meetings, games, projects, and outdoor events, including camping. You would work your way through an achievement handbook and receive a lively monthly magazine called *Dash*.

If you are in grades seven to twelve, you could join the Battalion program. Your achievement handbook would be *Brigade Trails*, but you could also choose from a selection of eighteen Skill Patch books,

covering topics like aviation, outdoor challenge, sports, or photography. You would receive *Venture* magazine.

For more information, or to find out if there is a church near you with this program, write: Christian Service Brigade, Box 150, Wheaton, Illinois 60187.

Christmas Sing-along

Do you like to listen to records?

Christmas is a great time of year for special music, and *The Christian Kids Almanac* especially recommends these Christmas albums:

Christmas Fever, Mayfield Youth Choir (Lillenas label). Here's a performance you can put on in your own church at Christmastime. This album contains seven original songs and a true-to-life story line. Other available items include songbook, and reel-to-reel and cassette tapes.

Christmas Around the World, Redwood Chapel Community Church Children's Choir, Castro Valley, California (Lillenas). A cantata of traditional carols from seven foreign countries, with brief narration telling the unique Christmas customs of each country. Also available: songbook with staging suggestions, reel-to-reel and cassette tapes, service folders, and orchestrations.

Psalty's Christmas Calamity, Kids Praise (Maranatha Music). This Christmas album includes traditional Christmas carols. Available in songbook and reel-to-reel and cassette tapes.

And your collection has to include one of the most popular Christmas albums of the decade, *Come On, Ring Those Bells* by Evie Tornquist Karlsson (Word). (See also *Evie*.)

Christmas Tree —Tallest

The world's tallest cut Christmas tree, according to the *Guinness Book of World Records,* was a 221-foot Douglas fir erected at Northgate Shopping Center in Seattle, Washington, in 1950. It was decorated all the way to the top with lights, too!

Circuit Riders

The American frontier beyond the Appalachian Mountains produced great heroes like Daniel Boone and Davy Crockett, but not far behind came another brand of heroes—the circuit riders.

These were preachers on horseback, who

roamed the wilderness in search of pioneers who needed to hear the gospel and Christians who needed encouragement.

Probably the most amazing circuit rider of them all was Francis Asbury. In the early 1800s, when thousands of pioneers left the East and trekked through the Cumberland Gap into the forests beyond, Asbury went after them.

Despite the peril of Indian attacks, the cold of winter, and the absence of roads, Asbury roamed the American wilderness for forty years. He planted the seeds of the gospel everywhere, and then came back year after year to examine the harvest.

It is said that Francis Asbury may have traveled more than one quarter million miles. And he preached some twenty-five thousand sermons!

Columbus, Christopher

What prompted Christopher Columbus to set out in treacherous waters into unknown seas? Those who write history say he had several motives: to serve God and the Church, to gain treasure and wealth, and to earn fame. The three G's: God, gold, and glory.

At the outset of his career, it seems that Columbus put service to God high in his life. He wrote, "I prayed to the most merciful Lord about my heart's great desire" (to sail the ocean westward), "and He gave me the spirit and the intelligence for the task."

He also wrote: "I am a most unworthy sinner, but I have cried out to the Lord for grace and mercy, and they have covered me completely. I have found the sweetest consolation since I made it my whole purpose to enjoy His marvelous presence. . . . No one should fear to undertake any task in the name of our Savior, if it is just. . . ."

The great drama of Columbus's voyage is

recorded in history. Days passed with no land in sight. Storms raged. His crew threatened mutiny. Though tempted again and again to turn back, he sailed on. Then, land at last!

Columbus saw the success of his voyage as a direct confirmation of God's will for his life. He saw his discovery as opening up new lands and tribes to the gospel. He called his first point of landing "San Salvador" (holy Savior).

Columbus returned to Spain a hero. His fame spread.

But then his great career started to collapse, for it was the gold and the glory that consumed him. As Columbus returned for his second and third and fourth voyages, things turned sour. On one voyage, Indians killed many of his crew. At another point Columbus himself wound up in chains, humiliated. He lost favor with his king and queen. Health problems plagued him.

At the close of his life, from the evidence of his own diary, he himself realized that he had drifted far from the Lord he had once served so gladly.

SEND FOR: Columbus Maps

Here are replicas of historical documents that look like the real thing. They are printed on parchment with a special process that gives them the look and texture of the original!

For just two dollars, you can receive:

1. *Map of Voyages of the New Continent 14th and 16th Centuries*, showing the four voyages of Columbus and the voyages of six other explorers.

2. *Declaration of Independence 1776*, a replica of the original.

3. *Lincoln's Gettysburg Address*, in his handwriting, with his signature.

Use these to decorate your room. Show them to your friends. Attach them to a school history report or theme paper.

For all three of these documents, send two dollars to: Historical Documents Company, Department CKA, 8 North Preston Street, Philadelphia, Pennsylvania 19104. (Price includes postage and handling.)

Computer in the Jungle

They call it the "Jungle Professor." What is it? Simply a computer in a suitcase that has now become the jungle missionary's best friend.

Around the world, thousands of missionaries have been working to translate the New Testament into the languages and dialects of remote jungle tribes. Each translation has usually taken at least ten years. But now the computers are saving months, even years, of this time.

They can be used to edit, type, analyze the language, revise transcripts, and create dictionaries of the language. The computer's memory becomes the missionary's "storage cabinet" or "file drawer" for almost everything he or she has learned about the language.

And if the missionary wants a printout of, say, the Epistle to the Romans, the "Jungle Professor" can produce it in just eight minutes!

Cross-Country Runners

In 1971, brothers Tony and Joel Ahlstrom ran cross-country from Long Beach, California, to Long Beach, New York—a distance of 2,905 miles. Along the way they testified of their faith in Jesus Christ and gathered signatures on antipollution legislation.

In 1976, they ran fifty-two miles a day, from the Golden Gate Bridge to the White House, carrying a Bible for President Gerald Ford and copies of the Declaration of Independence, with thousands of signatures from Americans they met along the way.

"I was always kind of an out-of-it kid," says Tony. "I was hopelessly cross-eyed. They tried a patch, glasses, machines, an operation. Nothing worked. And I was smaller than all the other kids. Besides that, my family was poor."

But that small "out-of-it" kid was determined not to give up on himself. He excelled in debate, won the state oratory championship in the tenth grade, and was elected student body president. After meeting the challenge of the cross-country run, Tony became a chaplain to the Chicago city council, under the regime of former mayor Michael Bilandic.

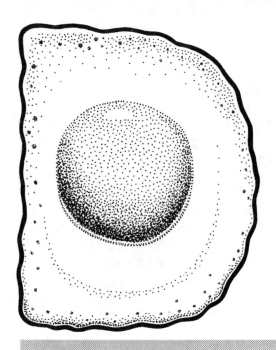

Days Inns

In 1968 an Atlanta real estate man named Cecil Day drove his family from Georgia to California. Along the way he had to pay hotel rates that he thought were too high for the average working man.

Once back from the family vacation, Day had his construction superintendent, Tom Fuqua, a devout Christian, design and build a sixty-unit motel on property at Georgia's Savannah Beach. It cost only four thousand dollars per unit, far below his competitors' building expenses. Within a year there were eight motels like it along interstates in the Southeast.

Already successful in real estate, Day had almost decided to retire. But friends urged him to pursue a full-scale motel plan. An Atlanta bank said they would finance the venture, but first they wanted the plan on paper.

But the ideas would not crystallize. That is, not until a business trip to Virginia, when Day awoke suddenly early one morning and began to write feverishly. Thirteen hours later he had the entire thesis for a motel empire that would eliminate the "frills" and bring low-cost overnight lodging to millions of American travelers. "The ideas were beyond my capabilities," Day later insisted. "It was God's leadership."

In line with his firm Christian convictions, Day refused to sell liquor in any of his motels, despite those who insisted that motels couldn't make a profit without it.

Today the Days Inns of America is still one of the fastest-growing and most economic motel chains in the nation.

FREE: Days Inns Directory

Obtain free the latest *Days Inns Directory* for your next family trip or vacation. Although many of these inns and lodges are in the South and East, the chain is now also expanding cross-country and into the western states. Write: Days Inns of America, Inc., 2751 Buford Highway N.E., Atlanta, Georgia 30324.

Dead Sea Scrolls

In 1947, a young Bedouin shepherd was climbing after a wandering goat along the craggy coast of the Dead Sea. He tossed a stone into one of the many hillside caves and heard an unexpected *clink:* the sound of pottery shattering.

Though he didn't realize it at the time, he had happened upon one of the greatest archaeological discoveries of the twentieth century. It was a treasure trove of scrolls, contained in earthen jars, which have since become known as the "Dead Sea scrolls." They had been stored in the caves by a Jewish community called Qumran, which the Romans destroyed in A.D. 69.

Why are the scrolls so important?

Because they contain, among other things, the complete scroll of the Old Testament Book of Isaiah—twenty-four feet long. The leather scroll was dated one thousand years earlier than any previously existing text. And the older such a scroll is, the closer it must be to the original scroll that all the others were copied from.

Scholars are still analyzing the Qumran scrolls, which include copies of all the Old Testament books but Esther. They have established that the Old Testament we have today, though passed down through the centuries, is essentially the same text as the ancient one the shepherd found. The Dead Sea Scrolls have proved to be a major piece of evidence that today's Bible is a faithful, accurate copy of the words God inspired his prophets and leaders to write.

If you ever go to Jerusalem, you can see fragments of the text, pieced together, on display at the Hebrew University. The fragments are protected under glass, and the exhibit can be lowered into the ground at night or in the event of enemy attack.

(For more on ancient finds, see *Archaeology, Lost Ark,* and *Ebla.*)

Demolition Expert

John Loizeaux (pronounced Lo-AH-zoh) blows up buildings all over the world. But no one has ever put him in jail for it! That's because he is not a terrorist.

People *ask* him to blow up their buildings!

On February 27, 1982, for instance, he blew up what had once been one of the most famous hotels in America: the historic old Cornhusker Hotel in Lincoln, Nebraska.

Thousands of citizens crowded the streets of downtown Lincoln to watch the dramatic event. Many more watched on television.

Miles of heavy cable had been wrapped around the ten-story structure. Charges of dynamite had been positioned in just the right places. Could John Loizeaux and his crack team of demolition experts bring the ten stories down without damage to the building right next to the hotel?

With everything ready, and crowds waiting, Loizeaux's crew ignited the dynamite. There was a great *boom!* Dust clouds flew. The hotel dropped straight downward and crumbled in upon itself. The people cheered!

Two days later John Loizeaux and his men were in Seattle, ready to bring down a twenty-two-story building. A delegation had flown all the way from Japan to observe the feat. Again, it was a success.

No one knows exactly how the world's foremost demolisher of buildings does it. Others can blow up buildings, but the explosion isn't always properly controlled or the building doesn't fall where it should. John Loizeaux has never seen anyone hurt. Nor has he damaged any surrounding properties, even in the tightest of situations.

His company has a few trade secrets, of course. But John Loizeaux gives credit for his success to the Lord. He is born again and not ashamed of it. For years his family has been associated with the Loizeaux line of Christian books.

Tearing down a building by the conventional method of swinging a ball on a crane can cost many millions and take months. John Loizeaux can do it in seconds! That means he often saves a firm millions of dollars. Sometimes he saves them so much that they want to give him a higher fee than he requests.

"No," he will say. "Put the investment back into your new building." As a man of thorough integrity, he knows this is the Christian thing to do.

Photo courtesy of Controlled Demolition, Inc.

Dial-a-Teen

When kids need help, other kids are sometimes the best ones to give it. Maybe that's why, in the Washington, D.C. area, at least a thousand calls a month pour in to Dial-a-Teen.

Kids call after hearing about Dial-a-Teen from friends, from articles in school papers, and from Dial-a-Teen radio and tv spots on more than two dozen local stations.

At Dial-a-Teen, all the counselors are Christian teenagers. They have all been through an intensive counselor-training course, and know how to apply the Bible to all kinds of situations.

Some who call are on drugs. Some threaten to take their own lives—like Beverly, whose friends, she said, made fun of her. The teen counselor on the other end of the line introduced her to Jesus, and that changed her life. (Dial-a-Teen plays a part in about one hundred decisions a month for Jesus Christ.)

When runaways call, they are referred to a toll-free number where experts stand ready to help.

Interested callers receive a Bible study course from Teen Missions, which initiated Dial-a-Teen (see *Teen Missions*), and one from Campus Crusade. They are also steered to good churches.

The service operates twenty-four hours a day, but calls for help are heaviest at night. And in snowstorms. Once when a heavy blizzard canceled school and work, an estimated eighty-eight thousand people tried to call in! The telephone company said the huge volume almost broke down service in that area.

The work of these Christian teens has even caught the attention of the White House. In 1981, Dial-a-Teen received a certificate of appreciation from President Ronald Reagan.

Dinosaur Valley

Near Glen Rose, Texas, the scenic Paluxy River flows over solid rock that contains the best preserved dinosaur tracks in Texas. If you visit Dinosaur Valley State Park, the Texas Parks and Wildlife Department will hand you a brochure stating that the dinosaurs there disappeared about one hundred million years ago, when this part of Texas was a long coastal plain.

Their tracks were embedded in the soft limey mud of this lush tropical region. Then, allegedly, land masses shifted, the climate changed, the lush vegetation gradually disappeared, and the age of the dinosaurs came to an end—long before man walked the area.

It's a standard explanation. But some of today's "scientific creationists" are not convinced that things happened in this time frame. In the same Paluxy riverbed, they call attention to some combinations of both dinosaur footprints and what appear to be human footprints.

The tracks occur in trails, and in two or three locations the dinosaur and human trails cross each other, with two cases where human and dinosaur tracks actually overlap each other.

What might this mean?

Simply that dinosaurs and man, according to this evidence, seem to have lived at the same time—not millions of evolutionary years apart. Dinosaurs, say these creationists, probably existed in relatively recent times.

The tracks have been documented in a film called *Footprints in Stone.* (See *Science Films.*)

What do you make of all this? It's up to you. You may want to read more about it, or visit Dinosaur Valley yourself.

Photo courtesy of Films for Christ

DNA

Have you ever tried to assemble a complex model? A gasoline engine? Or even sew a dress? If so, you know you have to put all the pieces together in the right order and arrangement.

So it is with the human body. Scientists have found that a complex chemical known as DNA carries "codes" for the human body that put it all together in orderly fashion. If you're wondering what DNA means, it stands for deoxyribonucleic acid. Aren't you glad you asked?

Riding on about six million genes, the chemical DNA will "program" such characteristics as your hair, eyes, skin, height. But this is only a start.

Your DNA code must also "program" the arrangement for:

- 206 bones,
- 100 billion nerve cells,
- 400 billion feet of blood vessels and capillaries,
- 600 muscles,
- 1 million optic nerve fibers for each eye,
- 5,000 auditory nerve fibers for each ear,
- and so on, and so on, and so on.

No wonder the Bible says we are "fearfully and wonderfully made" (Psalm 139: 14). Only God could arrange the incredible human body in proper working order.

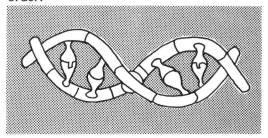

Dog's Best Friend

Nothing touches people's hearts more than a lonely puppy or kitten, looking for a home.

So when the Humane Society of Eureka Springs, Arkansas, said they could use a few more doghouses, a group of Pioneer Girls and their leaders decided to help. They built a village of ten doghouses, and each girl painted her name on a house.

They also designed some animal piggy banks and distributed them around town. From them they collected more than two hundred dollars to help the society feed and care for the animals. After that, they visited the shelter monthly to groom, clean, and love their new dog friends.

For these efforts the Humane Society, in a special ceremony, gave each Pioneer Girl an official membership card.

(See also *Pioneer Clubs.*)

These Arkansas girls made dogs' lives happier.

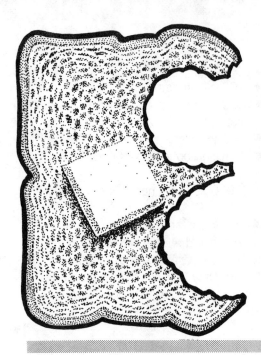

Easter Sunrise

Have you ever attended an outdoor Easter sunrise service? The most famous one in the country is held at the Hollywood Bowl. Such events are best suited to the climate of the West and the South. Elsewhere, at that time of year, you may still be trudging through snow!

But in Marion, Indiana, the weather never stops one of the most unusual Easter events in the United States. It's their annual Easter pageant, which transforms Marion's Memorial Coliseum into the streets of Jerusalem, and involves the talents of more than two thousand people—many of them kids. This includes more than five hundred working in makeup and costuming, a five-hundred-voice chorus, and a one-hundred-piece orchestra.

The one-hour pageant is unique in that no one in the cast speaks a word. The moving story of the last week of Jesus' life on earth is told entirely with pantomime, pageantry, and the music of great anthems and hymns.

Everyone who takes part remains anonymous, without fanfare or recognition—even the man who plays the lead role of Jesus. No names are mentioned, no salaries paid, no admission charged. The event calls attention only to the risen Lord!

Ebla

No doubt the name *Ebla* means nothing to you. But to many archaeologists around the world, it means "the find of the century." Some regard it as even greater than the discovery of the scrolls at Qumran (see *Dead Sea Scrolls*).

An Italian archaeologist discovered the buried city of Ebla in northern Syria in 1964. Careful analysis has revealed it to be

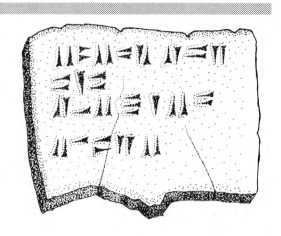

the seat of a mighty empire that had flourished around 2400 B.C.

Christian scholars are especially excited about the sixteen thousand cuneiform tablets found in Ebla's ancient library. The tablets contain references to numerous people and places mentioned in the Bible.

For example, the tablets mention the cities of Sodom and Gomorrah, which the Bible says God destroyed because of their sin. Some critics of the Bible had insisted that cities like these didn't even exist.

(For more about ancient finds, see *Archaeology* and *Lost Ark*.)

Elvis's Stepbrother

Almost every young boy or girl dreams of fame and fortune—or at least of being around someone famous.

Rick Stanley can tell you about it first-hand. As the stepbrother of rock 'n' roll star Elvis Presley, he moved into the star's home, Graceland Mansion, when only five years old.

The next eighteen years were filled with money, cars, travel, and famous friends.

At eighteen Rick was Elvis's personal aide and bodyguard, hopping from city to city. The crowds screamed. The two met other famous entertainers.

But Rick Stanley wasn't happy. And drugs and alcohol only made his life worse.

There was one person, though, that he couldn't get out of his mind. She was Robyn Moye, an old high school friend who had been telling him about the Lord for a long time.

One day he told Elvis about the girl. "She's been telling me about Jesus for seven years," he said, "and this time it really hit home."

"Rick, you know that young girl is right," said Elvis. "It's about time we all started living for God."

But only hours later, Elvis Presley was found dead at Graceland Mansion.

A short time later, Rick Stanley turned his life over to Jesus. Everyone saw a sudden change. For hours each day, he studied the Bible. Then he decided to go to a Bible institute and to become an evangelist.

Eventually he married—guess who? Robyn, who had led him to the Lord. Rick and Robyn now speak to young people across the country.

"There's a world of Rick Stanleys out there right now," Rick tells them. "They are people who are messed up on drugs, alcohol, running around looking for peace of mind. They need Jesus."

Rick acted as Elvis's bodyguard and personal aide.

Evie

For several years now kids have ranked Evie (Tornquist) Karlsson among their favorite gospel singers. *Record World* voted her the top female gospel artist in America. She has appeared in Carnegie Hall, performed for the king of Norway, and sung for the president of the United States.

Evie has sung since she was tiny. She sang duets with her mother in churches all around New Jersey when she was only three! But her career didn't take off till she was fourteen, and then it was almost by accident. She was visiting Norway with her parents, who are native Norwegians. The leader of a camp she was attending asked her if she would sing some gospel music for the crowd at a camp meeting. Even though Evie was wearing grubby jeans and a T-shirt and her hair was still wet from swimming, she gladly agreed to perform.

It just so happened that a member of the audience was a director of a national television program. After her performance, he asked her to appear on his talk show. Evie sang three songs on the program and chatted comfortably with the other guests—a breath of fresh air in the stiff formality of Scandinavian television. Her tv appearance triggered a deluge of offers inviting her to sing. She accepted eighty of them, and her career was on its way.

During the next years of her high school days in Rahway, New Jersey, Evie seemed like any other American teenager, toting books and doing homework. But every fourth week she spent abroad in places like Norway, Sweden, Denmark, and Holland, giving concerts and appearing on tv. The young performer's fame spread first from Scandinavia and other parts of Europe to Canada, and from there to the United States, as well as Australia.

Evie has refused to compromise her personal Christian convictions for the sake of broader success. She has turned down offers from record companies that wanted her to include some secular songs in her repertoire, because she does not wish to do so. She has declined invitations to appear on talk shows in the United States that required her to sing only pop songs.

Two of her more recent works are the chart-topping *Mirror*, and *Unfailing Love. A Little Song of Joy for My Little Friends*, also popular, was recorded especially for children, and contains songs both old and new. It's the fruit of an idea which Evie, always popular with children, has had for years.

In 1978 Evie married Swedish pastor and composer Pelle Karlsson. The Karlssons make their home in Sweden, and are seeking ways to combine their gifts for God's service.

"God has no celebrities in his family," Evie has written. "He has only children. No one person has a more prestigious position than another in God's family. We are all servants."

Photo courtesy of Word Records

Ezekiel Airship

Just about everyone learns in school that the Wright brothers flew the first airplane at Kitty Hawk, North Carolina, in 1903.

But down in northeast Texas, many folks think that a Baptist pastor may have been one step ahead of the Wrights.

In the small town of Pittsburg, northwest of Longview, Texas, a historical marker reads:

The Ezekiel Airship

Baptist minister and inventor Burrell Cannon (1848-1922) led some Pittsburg investors to establish the Ezekiel Airship Company and build a craft described in the Book of Ezekiel. The ship had large, fabric-covered wings powered by an engine that turned four sets of paddles. It was built in a nearby machine shop (still standing) and was briefly airborne at this site late in 1902, a year before the Wright brothers first flew. En route to the St. Louis World's Fair in 1904, the airship was destroyed by a storm. In 1913 a second model crashed, and the Rev. Cannon gave up the project.

The designer's engineering concepts included an inner wheel within each of the machine's four main wheels, which went one half revolution backward for each revolution forward by the main wheel. The Reverend Cannon got his "wheel within a wheel" inspiration from the Bible, and for fifty cents offered potential stockholders an eight-by-ten-inch photo of the airship plus an explanation of the first and tenth chapters of Ezekiel.

Evidence seems to establish that the plane rose about ten feet off the ground and flew more than 160 feet, but drifted to one side into a fence and came down in a pasture.

Was it under control during the flight? Did its inventor technically "fly" the first airplane?

The world will probably never know.

Rev. Cannon had this drawing of the Ezekiel Airship printed on his stockholders' certificates.

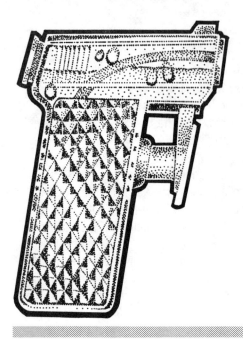

Fame

Raymond Berry, a forthright Christian and former powerhouse for the Cleveland Browns, at one time had to have police protection simply to exit from the field— because of the crush of all his fans.

Some years later he was leisurely autographing a ball for a small boy. An onlooker asked why he was taking so long.

"I'm making the most of it," Berry quipped. "It's only the third request I've had this year!"

"Fame! I'm gonna live forever," says the theme song from the movie *Fame* and the subsequent tv series. But it's not necessarily true. The celebrated tv star loses his show's prime-time slot to another with better ratings, and fades into obscurity. The ballplayer retires from sports and goes into private life. The prominent political figure loses the election. After a while, people forget former celebrities.

Maybe you have had that forgotten, abandoned, "nobody" feeling. You make a great play in a ball game one week, and you're a hero. The next week you bobble the ball, and everyone's down on you.

Just remember that, as God sees you, you're always a VIP. You are God's child— today, tomorrow, and forever!

Fellowship of Christian Athletes

This organization was the first to create a Christian ministry especially geared to athletes. Founded in 1954, the FCA works with athletes from the pro level to college and high school, and now is also becoming active at the junior high level. It runs "huddle" groups for prayer, Bible study, and discussion at two thousand high schools, five hundred junior highs, and three hundred colleges, sponsored by individual coaches and teachers at each school. The FCA also holds summer sports conferences ("inspiration and perspiration") for about ten thousand boys and girls each year.

For more information about the camps or about a "huddle" for your school, write to: Fellowship of Christian Athletes, 8701 Leeds Road, Kansas City, Missouri 64129.

Films for Kids: Award Winners

One fun and interesting way to learn more about the Christian faith today is to watch one of the many Christian films now available. *The Christian Kids Almanac* has listed some of the best general ones here, and there are also movies listed under *Sci-*

The Lion, the Witch and the Wardrobe. This Emmy Award-winning film has been shown on CBS Network Television. Adapted from the classic by C. S. Lewis, it conveys the death and resurrection of Christ through the use of allegory. Distributed by Gospel Films (110 minutes).

The Great Banana Pie Caper (Quadrus). Named "Best Children's Film" in 1979 by Christian Film Distributors. Theodore and

The mess has just begun for Theodore and Mason in The Great Banana Pie Caper.

Photo courtesy of Quadrus Communications

ence *Films* and *Sports Films.* Someone at your church may want to rent one of these for you and your friends—or the whole church family.

Mason bake and attempt to deliver seventy-five banana cream pies—while being pursued by a gang of bullies. The wild bicycle chase has hilarious results. For children through junior high age (28 minutes).

The Mystery of Willoughby Castle (Quadrus). "Best Children's Film" of 1980. Three youngsters, exploring Willoughby Castle, stumble onto revolving bookcases that lead to hidden passageways and a secret laboratory with bizarre inventions. Animated, for children through junior high age (35 minutes).

Tanglewood's Secret (Glenray). From a Moody Press novel by Patricia St. John. Ruth and Philip build their own wigwam in the woods to play in, and one day find a gypsy boy inside. Soon all are in danger. Named "Best Motion Picture" (Angel Award) by Religion in Media in Hollywood, and given an award of excellence at the International Film Festival in Holland (80 minutes).

Humpty (Glenray). Humpty is the only white egg in a kingdom of colored eggs—and proud of it. The king forbids any of the eggs to venture beyond the great wall, where evil lurks, but Humpty can't resist. This animated film won first place at the International Film Festival & Exposition in Philadelphia, and was given a Golden Halo Award by the Southern California Motion Picture Council (25 minutes).

The Paradise Trail (Mark IV Pictures). Some have called this unusual film "the first Christian western." A blind pastor and his wife are held captive by two outlaw brothers, whose threats do not deter the couple from sharing the message of God's love and forgiveness. Tension mounts as the outlaws respond to the gospel in opposite ways. Awarded "Best Soul Winning Film" (69 minutes).

The Goosehill Gang and the Mystery of the Treehouse Ghost (Family Films). "Best Children's Film" of 1982. Michael thinks the gang's old oak tree, and the treehouse in it, is haunted (20 minutes).

Films: Real People

If you like true stories, you should know that some of today's Christian films bring you right into people's lives. Here are ten films about "real people" that *The Christian Kids Almanac* recommends.

A Circle of Love (Song Vision). This film takes you behind the scenes with singer Amy Grant (see *Amy*), whose popular Christian music includes "My Father's Eyes," "Faith Walkin' People," "Giggle," and "Old Man's Rubble." Filmed on location in Nashville and Atlanta.

Ann's Kids . . . in the Holyland (Gospel Films). Popular writer Ann Kiemel walks and talks with children through the settings of many Old and New Testament events. She continually reminds her kids that both the places and the people who lived the stories in the Bible are not fictitious, not

Peace Child takes you into a Stone Age tribe.

Photo courtesy of Gospel Films

part of a fairy tale. They were real people, who lived in real places, doing real things, just as the Bible says.

Barrett (Outreach Films). The life of Sergeant Gary Barrett, a Los Angeles area cop, who lives face-to-face with danger every day—and knows that God helps him through life-and-death situations. Gary Barrett, by the way, is the son of Ethel Barrett, nationally known for her great story-telling abilities with children.

The Conversion of Colonel Bottomly (Family Films). In the middle of the Vietnam War, the career of jet pilot Heath Bottomly, U.S. Air Force colonel, was on its way to the top. Then suddenly disaster struck.

When Colonel Bottomly saw a buddy of his shot out of the air by the Communists, he crossed the "no strike zone," against the orders of President Lyndon Johnson, to retaliate. The colonel was promptly court-martialed. His career dreams shattered, the distraught colonel telephoned his son, a Christian, who was fifteen thousand miles away at Purdue University in Indiana. The ending will surprise you.

The Cross and the Switchblade (Gateway). Based on David Wilkerson's outreach

Christ. Starring Pat Boone and Erik Estrada.

The Devil's Coach (Outreach Films). The story of Jim Brock, coach of the championship Arizona State University Sun Devils baseball team. (See also *Sports Films*.)

Heaven's Heroes (Mark IV). The true story of a Christian policeman, Dennis Hill, who is killed in an ambush.

Hudson Taylor (Ken Anderson Films). The story of mainland China's famous pioneer missionary. A truly epic motion picture with spectacular costumes and scenery. For older youth.

Jill (Quadrus). Jill, a talented, attractive Christian girl, learns she has terminal cancer, and has only months to live. Despite the circumstances, her life is calm and joyous. A true story, starring the real Jill, with film footage taken before her death.

Peace Child (Gospel Films). The true and remarkable story of missionaries Don and Carol Richardson, filmed in the unspoiled

The Cross and the Switchblade *(left) tells of a street gang;* Heaven's Heroes *(right) of a Christian policeman.*

Photo courtesy of Mark IV Films

to street gangs in New York City. At first Wilkerson fails miserably in his effort to lead embittered kids away from a life of drugs and violence. But the breakthrough comes when Nicky Cruz, leader of the notorious Mau-Mau's, gives his life to

jungles of the southwest Pacific. You will see how the message of Jesus transforms Stone Age people, and be amazed at the strange custom that helped them understand Christianity's central truth. Excellent cinematography.

"First" Ladies

The first white women to cross the Rockies were Christian missionaries Narcissa Whitman and Eliza Spaulding (see *Oregon Trailblazers*).

The first woman to become a jet pilot in the United States Air Force was a Christian housewife, Connie Engel (see *Jet Pilot*).

The first woman doctor was Elizabeth Blackwell, the daughter of a wealthy sugar merchant from England, whose family came to America in 1833 to escape religious persecution. Despite tremendous odds, Elizabeth pursued her dream of a medical career, convinced God had called her to it.

The Blackwell family fortune collapsed when Elizabeth's father refused to accept America's slave system and have his sugarcane cut cheaply by black slaves. But Elizabeth overcame the financial odds, and finally found a medical school that would let her in—the first woman ever to be accepted. Despite some harassment by townspeople and by other medical students, she received her medical degree in 1849. Later, in New York City, she founded the nation's first women's medical college.

And, while we're on first ladies, you should know that the very first pilot to fly for the Missionary Aviation Fellowship (MAF) was a woman: pioneer missionary aviationist Betty Greene.

Together with a group of former Navy jet jockeys, she was flying missionary supplies over the steep mountain gorges of Borneo's interior, beginning in 1946. She flew for thirty-four years, and only recently retired.

Betty can tell you all kinds of hair-raising stories—like the one about the time she was landing on a rugged mountaintop in New Guinea with a Dani tribesman in the backseat. Just at a critical moment in the descent, the aborigine's hand reached over Betty's shoulder and grabbed the throttle! It took all of her skills to undo the damage. In a split second, with her feet hard against the rudder pedals, she readjusted the throttle and kept the plane from plunging over a precipice.

The tribesman, only recently removed from a Stone Age existence, meant no harm. In his society, men allowed women to do only the most menial of tasks. So in this case, the tribesman simply felt it was his duty to bring down the plane himself!

Flight Pin

You may never have seen it before, but some airline pilots and flight attendants wear gold pins on their lapels in the design you see here.

They belong to the Fellowship of Christian Airline Personnel (FCAP). The movement was started in the early 1970s by a Delta Airlines pilot in Atlanta and a United Airlines pilot in Chicago.

Those who wear the FCAP pin say it helps identify them to other Christian believers and also invites opportunities to explain its meaning.

And just what does the pin mean?

The global background indicates God's concern for the whole world. Note also the jet aircraft and a "runway" in the shape of a cross. The aircraft symbolizes the people associated with the airline industry, and the runway points to Jesus Christ's death on the cross, the way to heaven for all who accept him as Savior.

Flood Theory

Did the Flood of which the Bible speaks really cover the whole earth? Or just a small part of it—the known world, the area of the Mediterranean?

Christians hold different views on this. The idea of a "smaller" Flood, at least at first, may not seem as hard to believe. After all, if the Flood covered the entire earth, where did all the water come from?

But here is how scientific creationists who believe in a "universal" Flood explain it—and a few other things as well:

In the beginning a thick vapor canopy, they theorize, covered the earth. The whole earth was lush and warm like a greenhouse. There were no deserts and no ice caps. Mist and dew watered the earth.

Suddenly the vapor canopy collapsed. Waters poured down from the sky. Even greater quantities of water bubbled up from within the crust of the earth.

This catastrophic event vastly altered the surface of the earth. In a short time, as the Flood waters receded into what are today's oceans, much of today's geological forma-

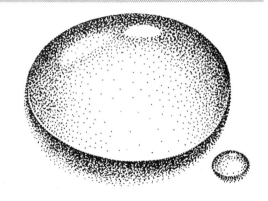

tions were built. Slower processes since then modify the earth's features.

The extremes of climate that we know today emerged because there was no longer a "vapor canopy," these scientists claim. The collapse of the vapor canopy also shortened the life span of man, because much greater amounts of radiation reached earth from outer space than ever before.

Is this vapor canopy theory right? As you grow and learn, you will have to decide whether or not you think there is adequate scientific evidence for the view. Maybe you can even do research on the topic.

Football Prayer?

Astronaut Jack Lousma, who commanded the successful *Columbia* space shuttle flight in March 1982, once asked God to help him do his best in a high school football game.

He scored five touchdowns!

The next week he repeated his request for divine help. And he played the worst game of his career!

Jack Lousma later realized that he needed to thank God for the great game, not take all of the credit for himself. He had learned something.

It's a healthy habit to pray before a game, either on your own or as a team. But don't count on your prayer to assure a win. God may have other lessons to teach you!

(Note: For another look at Jack Lousma the astronaut, see *Space Shuttle*.)

Football Profiles

Bob Breunig
Middle Linebacker, Dallas Cowboys

Bob Breunig is one of the most intense, disciplined players Dallas coach Tom Landry says he has ever met. As middle linebacker for the Cowboys since 1977, he has helped them win the Super Bowl, and in 1981 his

Photo courtesy of the Dallas Cowboys

peers voted him NFL starting middle linebacker in the Pro Bowl.

Until his senior year at Arizona State University, Bob Breunig says he wasn't really satisfied with his life, despite success, friends, and no shortage of parties. But then he turned himself over to the Lord, and life began to make sense. He started to read the Bible, and he began to realize that everything he did had to be for a purpose—even playing football.

In an interview with Al Janssen for *Young Ambassador* magazine, he said, "Football is a contact sport, but it isn't a kill sport. As a Christian, my outlook is to play fair, to play by the rules, and to play as hard as I can—not to impress anyone else, but to say thank you to God for the talents and the healthy body he's given me."

(For more on the Cowboys, see *Landry, Tom*.)

Steve Largent
Wide Receiver, Seattle Seahawks

Remember the National Football League's 1982 strike? The players refused to play until they got a better contract. Most of them, that is.

Steve Largent of the Seattle Seahawks, one of the top receivers in the NFL, felt

Football Profiles,
continued

obligated as a Christian to honor his contract. "God's Word calls a contract a vow," he said. "I've made a vow with the Seahawks that I will play football with them for three more years. To break that vow would be wrong."

It was not a popular stand with some of the other players; even other Christians did not necessarily agree with Steve. But he knew it was important to do what *he* felt was right in God's eyes. In the end, most of the players respected his courage.

During the off season, Largent often works at a football camp for junior high boys. He has also worked with high school teens in Young Life. It was while he was a sophomore in high school, in fact, that Steve made his decision for Jesus Christ.

Jeff Siemon
Linebacker, Minnesota Vikings

Many people rely on the applause of others to make them feel worthwhile—especially athletes.

"I attempted to gain my sense of self-worth and self-esteem through the eyes of others," admitted Jeff Siemon of the Minnesota Vikings when he remembered his growing-up years.

But at Stanford University, Siemon suffered a severe knee injury during his freshman football season, and the doctors said he might never play the game again. His self-esteem suddenly dropped.

It took a letter from a Christian girl friend, and the witness of a campus Christian worker going door to door through the dormitories, to turn him to the God who loved him, even when he was just another freshman watching football instead of playing. Months later his knee healed up much better than the doctors had dreamed, and he was able to return to the playing field.

After Jeff Siemon became a Christian, he and a handful of other Christians on the Stanford team began to make an impact on their teammates. Before long, football chapel services grew from five players to forty-five! During that time Siemon also played a major role in Stanford's upsets of Big Ten powers Michigan and Ohio State in the 1971 and 1972 Rose Bowls.

Siemon was the Vikings' first-round draft pick in 1972. He claims that his faith makes a big difference in his football today. "I used to get so nervous and psyched up preparing for big games that I couldn't really perform adequately," he remembers. "My relationship with Christ helps release me from the tremendous emotional burden I used to place upon myself."

Photo courtesy of the Minnesota Vikings

Frontier Camp Meetings

In the early days of Kentucky, Christians staged one of the largest "camp-outs" of all time.

It all started when some frontier preachers joined forces to evangelize settlers in the wilderness. God's Spirit was at work, and the crowds grew. Kentuckians from as far as one hundred miles away began to thread their way to the meetings in Logan County, not far from where tourists today visit the Mammoth Caves.

Some visitors had to camp out for one, two, or three nights. Men chopped down trees to accommodate the growing crowds, and arranged split-log benches into pews for what might be called an outdoor church. People gathered in clusters around various ministers, who preached from stumps and logs instead of pulpits.

One writer describes the impressive scene at night: "The glare of campfires . . . long ranges of tents . . . hundreds of candles and lamps suspended among the trees . . . the solemn chanting of hymns swelling and falling on the night wind . . . earnest prayers . . ."

A great meeting at Cane Ridge near Lexington in August 1801 climaxed it all. The famous gathering, called the "Second Great Awakening," extended over several days and drew crowds estimated as high as twenty-five thousand—an incredible figure in view of the sparse population of the frontier at that time.

The preachers who staged the event at Cane Ridge had counted on a large buffalo herd nearby to provide meat for those who came. But the crowds were so great that the buffalo fled! Food ran out, and the crowds finally had to return home.

The format of camp meetings like this laid the foundation for the evangelistic crusades and campaigns that are more familiar today.

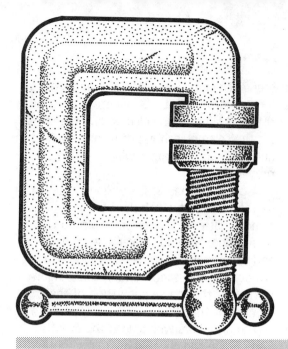

Gallup Poll

Almost everyone has heard of the Gallup polls. They tell us current public opinion: what people are thinking, how they plan to vote, and more.

George Gallup, Jr., who directs the complex survey network that his father founded, is a man who loves Jesus.

That's why, a few years ago, he decided to use some of his survey machinery to help find out what people think about religion, churches, the Bible, and God.

He found some interesting facts, including facts about young people.

• Most Americans (93 percent) said they believe that Jesus Christ rose from the dead.

• Most parents said they would like to see their children in Sunday school.

• A lot of people of all ages don't go to church—but would if they were only asked!

• U.S. youth rank among the most religious in the world. While 41 percent of young Americans say they think religion should be "very important" in life, merely 8 to 12 percent of the young people in Europe say this. Only in the Philippines (83 percent), India (60 percent), and Brazil (52

percent) are higher proportions recorded.

• Japanese youth are the most likely to say they have no religious belief—70 percent—while young people in Brazil are the least likely to say so.

• Forty-six percent of Protestant teenagers say thay are born again, as do 22 percent of Catholic teens.

• Seventy-one percent among the "born again" group say they have tried to encour-

age someone to believe in Jesus Christ or accept him as Savior.

- While almost every home has a Bible, teens don't read it. Only one in ten, the survey showed, reads the Bible daily.

- Teens in the South and Midwest read the Bible more often than teens in the East and West. Here are the survey figures on the number of teens who said they read the Bible at least once a week: in the East, 20 percent; the Midwest, 36 percent; the South, 47 percent; and the West, 30 percent.

Garfield, James

"Ready, you hoggee? . . . Cast off!" Captain Letcher yelled from the front of the canalboat.

Jim Garfield slapped the reins, stirring his horses to a slow walk on the towpath alongside the Erie Canal. The towline stretched tight, and the canalboat began moving silently through the water.

James Garfield was the only U.S. president who was also a preacher—and a good one at that! But when he was a teenager, no one expected Jim to be more than a rough-and-tough sailor on the Erie Canal.

For two years, James Garfield walked the towpath of the Erie Canal as a hoggee, a driver of the team of horses that pulled the canalboats. Sometimes he was ambushed by bullies from towns alongside the canal. Other times he was hassled by other hoggees.

Finally, Jim became restless and dissatisfied with his life. He knew that the friends he had made weren't doing him any good. Because of their rough and dangerous existence, they drank and used profane language, two habits that were beginning to become a part of his own life-style.

When a camp meeting came to his hometown of Chagrin Falls, Ohio, Garfield decided to attend. On March 3, 1850, he opened his heart to the Lord, and the next day he was baptized in the ice-cold waters of the Chagrin River. When he was still in his early twenties, Garfield preached both in churches and at revival meetings.

At Williams College in Massachusetts, Garfield also took an open stand for the Lord. At the end of the school's annual "Mountain Day Frolic" and climb of Mount Greylock, the students assembled to celebrate with some alcoholic beverages. They turned to Garfield to lead them in the festivities. Instead, James Garfield pulled a bat-

This illustration—and the first two paragraphs of this article—come from Canal Boy, *published by David C. Cook.*

tered Bible from his pocket and told them it was his habit to read a chapter from the Bible every evening. "Shall I read aloud?" he asked.

Then there was the time Garfield took on an atheist by the name of Denton in a series of public debates on the subject of evolution. His foe was a rapid, elegant, fiery speaker who had argued the subject in public forty times. To prepare himself, Garfield crammed for weeks in geology, physiology, and other sciences.

The debate ran for five days, with two sessions a day. Hundreds, even thousands, turned out. Denton tried his best to invalidate the claims of the Bible and "remove God from immediate control of the universe." But Garfield countered his opponent at every turn, point for point.

By all accounts, Denton's stand had been demolished by the time the debate was over.

Garfield was elected president in 1880 by a slim margin. But he was shot after only half a year in office, and lingered several more months before dying.

What sort of president would he have been if he had not been assassinated? No one knows.

FREE: Garfield Stamp For a free U.S. postage stamp that depicts President James Garfield and was printed more than a half century ago, write: Robert Flood, *The Christian Kids Almanac,* David C. Cook Publishing, 850 North Grove Avenue, Elgin, Illinois 60120. Include twenty-five cents for postage and handling.

Gem Carvings

Some kids collect rocks. Some grown-ups do, too. Some polish their rocks for display. And some carve precious stones into beautiful art objects. A gem carver is called a lapidary.

Olive Colhour is the leading lapidary artist in the world. She has traveled around the world with her exhibits, lectured, and appeared on television. Her collection is worth 1.5 million dollars!

When she carves flowers, with tools she designed herself, they look incredibly real. A spray of roses looks as though someone just picked it from the garden—drops of dew still clinging to the paperlike leaves. Spectators sometimes lean forward to sniff the fragrance before they realize that the flowers are made of coral, the leaves of jade, and the dewdrops of quartz!

Olive Colhour did not even discover the

These roses are made of coral, the leaves of jade, the stems and thorns of jasper, and the dewdrops of quartz crystal.

hobby that made her famous until age fifty-seven, when she decided to fix up her fireplace with a face of quartz crystals. "I simply went to a rock club to find out what to do with my crystals," she says. That started it all. She is now eighty-five.

There's something more you should know about Olive Colhour. She has always seen a direct link between her artistry and her relationship to God.

"When I am working on a project," she says, "I truly feel as if I am in the presence of God. He gave this collection to me, so I must give it to others."

Now she has given a large part of her collection to Crista Ministries, a Christian organization geared to help people in need, especially the young, the elderly, the troubled, and the poor. The gems are on display in their Seattle headquarters.

"George Washington Sat Here"

When George Washington took office as the first president of the United States, it was not in Washington, D.C. The first capital of the United States was New York City.

The church where George Washington worshiped is on the corner of New York's Broadway and Fulton Streets. His pew, bearing the Great Seal of the United States above it, is still preserved.

As the first president, Washington was at a distinct political disadvantage. He could not blame the problems of the nation on the previous administration!

Geronimo!

For kids playing war, the shout of "Geronimo!" is the sure signal for an attack.

The expression comes from the famed Apache chief Geronimo, who spent years taking vengeance on the white man for the murder of Apache families.

There's more to the story.

After Geronimo and his tribe surrendered to the U.S. army in 1886, the Apaches were put on an Oklahoma reservation—contrary to the treaty. There the bitter Geronimo attended classes at a mission, and heard the gospel.

In 1903 Geronimo was baptized and joined the Fort Sill church. He learned to live peaceably with the white man. He even endured being "exhibited" before crowds at the 1904 World's Fair in St. Louis. Geronimo practiced Christlike love and self-sacrifice until his death in 1909 at age seventy-nine.

Glass Cathedral

The "Crystal Cathedral" in Garden Grove, California, not far from Disneyland, is built with ten thousand panels of glass! It is longer than a football field and more than 120 feet high. A sparkling fountain runs down the main aisle!

The church—really named the Garden Grove Community Church—has ten thousand members. Its pastor, Robert Schuller, started the congregation twenty-five years ago, when he preached his first sermon on Easter Sunday from the roof of a nearby drive-in theater—to just a handful of people in a few cars. More than 225,000 visitors, many of them vacation travelers, tour the church each year.

Golden Gate

The photo you see below shows what is called the Golden Gate in the east wall of Jerusalem.

This wall was probably built in the seventh century, but it is believed to stand on the foundation stones of the gate that Jesus triumphantly entered a few days before he was crucified.

Now, do you notice anything strange about what you see?

Yes, the entrance is walled up.

Take a quick look in your Bible at Ezekiel 44:2, and you will read these words: "Then said the Lord unto me; this gate shall be shut, it shall not be opened, and no man shall enter in by it; because the Lord, the God of Israel, hath entered in by it, therefore it shall be shut."

For more than fifteen hundred years it appeared as though this prophecy would go unfulfilled.

But in 1543, Sultan Suleiman the Magnificent found that most of the Jerusalem wall had been destroyed—except for this gate. He set out to rebuild it. But since the road from the Kidron Valley up the hill to this particular gate was no longer usable, he changed his mind and ordered his workmen to seal it shut.

It remains shut to this day.

Photo courtesy of Biblical Archaeology Review

Golf Links

Each week during the annual PGA (Professional Golfers' Association) Tour, 144 golfers tee up on Thursday for the chance to be the winner four days later. Some players are new to the tour; some are veterans of many years. Some are well-known tournament winners, whose names you would recognize. Others are "rabbits," trying to qualify each Monday for a new tournament, struggling just to remain on the tour.

Each player competes against himself and the field. The lure of the links brings them together. Yet despite the competition, a group of these men have banded together in another "link": their common bond in Jesus Christ.

These players have formed a PGA tour Bible study. Each week anywhere from fifteen to thirty players and their wives meet to study the Bible and discuss their lives in the community of Jesus Christ.

Gary Player, who won the U.S. Open in 1965, is among the regulars. "Man needs to serve a higher purpose than just winning golf tournaments," he says.

Also among them is Larry Nelson, who in 1979 came within a hair of winning the World Series of Golf. (A buried lie in the bunker caused him to double bogey the 17th hole, and that cost him the championship.) The difference between first and second place was sixty-four thousand dollars! That night, quite understandably, Nelson tossed in his bed for a couple of hours, thinking of what had happened. But then he remembered one of his favorite Bible passages, Philippians 4:6, 7: "Do not be anxious about anything . . ." As he prayed, he began to feel the peace God promises in the verse.

The key catalyst of the PGA Bible studies, however, has been Rik Massengale, who got them going several years ago, following his own conversion to Christ. (If you're a golf fan, you may remember that Rik won the Bob Hope Desert Classic in 1977 with a record 23 under par.) Other regulars at the studies include Bob Gilder, Wally Armstrong, and Doug Tewll.

FRANKLY GEORGE, A GOLF COURSE IN CALIFORNIA DOESN'T SEEM TO BE THE PLACE TO TALK ABOUT RELIGION. . . .

Good News and Bad News

One day in 1982, the thirteen hundred students of Chicago's Moody Bible Institute joined hands and entirely circled their campus. The line stretched for about twelve city blocks. Then the students prayed together for their school.

Since the school is on a busy traffic intersection, just north of Chicago's "Loop" center, hundreds of passing motorists stared in amazement at the scene.

The school promptly received a call from a city journalist. "What's going on over there?" he asked, sensing a hot story. "Is it a protest or something?"

The reporter was told that the students were praying for their school and for the impact of its missionaries around the world.

"Oh," he said. And hung up.

The reporter wasn't interested. He didn't understand it. Also, it was good news. He was apparently looking for bad news.

One evening shortly after the incident just described, two girls from Moody Bible Institute were walking near their campus when they found a wallet in the middle of a busy intersection. The girls promptly turned it in to the nearest police station. It contained $380.

When the man who had lost the wallet reported it, the police told him, to his great surprise, where he could pick it up. The man was sure that, even if the wallet were found, the money would be gone. But it wasn't! The man gave fifty dollars to the girls who had turned it in, and praised them highly for their honesty.

The *Chicago Tribune* got wind of the story and ran it, with a photo of the girls, on its front page. This time there was a reporter who recognized the value of good news.

If you like to write, and should ever become a journalist, be sure not to ignore all the good news.

Gospel Music Hall of Fame

A "Gospel Music Hall of Fame" is on the drawing boards for Nashville, Tennessee. It was originally to have been built directly across the street from the Country Music Hall of Fame, but the site has now been changed.

Although some of today's "Nashville Sound" has gone electronic, much of country music had its roots in the gospel sounds of Appalachia. It is no surprise, then, that Nashville is also the religious recording capital of the world.

The original Grand Ole Opry House in Nashville, known as the Ryman Auditorium, still draws sightseers. But in its early days, the building was a gospel tabernacle for famed evangelist Sam Jones. Later the building was named for Tom Ryman, one of Jones's most dynamic converts.

That was many years ago, but God is still at work in the lives of some of Nashville's celebrities. James Hefley's book, *How Sweet the Sound* (Tyndale House), tells the behind-the-scenes stories of the struggles and triumphs of Grand Ole Opry stars.

(See also *Mandrell, Barbara*.)

Graham, Ruth

You may think that preachers and their wives are stuffy, boring sorts of people. But Ruth Bell Graham (Mrs. Billy Graham) is the adventurous, outdoor type who has had her share of thrills and spills.

Her evangelist husband, Billy Graham, said of her not long ago, "She loves to ride motorcycles. When hang gliding came along, she took hang gliding lessons. I came home one day and she was black-and-blue. She had fallen in one of her hang gliding escapades."

Only a few years ago she climbed a tree in Milwaukee to fix a Chinese swing for her grandchildren. (As the daughter of missionaries, Ruth Graham was born and raised in China.) She jumped out to test it—and fell fourteen feet to the ground. The mishap put Mrs. Graham in the hospital for ten weeks!

Another interest of Mrs. Graham's is writing poetry. Her recent book of poems, *Sitting by My Laughing Fire,* includes some poems from her teen years in the Far East.

For some information on her husband, see *Billy's Birthplace.*

Grand Canyon

A family vacation in the West very often includes the Grand Canyon. Millions of tourists over the years have stood on its rim and stared in awe at its beauty.

Because the canyon cuts into the surface of the earth up to almost a mile in depth, it has given geologists a dramatic look at a cross section of the earth's crust.

For years evolutionists have looked upon the Grand Canyon as their "Exhibit A." For one thing, they say it was formed slowly, over at least sixty million years, as the Colorado River gradually cut deeper and deeper through the rock. And this fits with the age of the earth as they perceive it.

Today some scientists have begun to challenge this explanation. They think that the Grand Canyon did not emerge from millions of years of gradual erosion, but

Photo courtesy of the National Park Service

from the sudden catastrophe of a great flood. This theory says the canyon formed while sediments were still soft from the flood, and while waters were receding off the face of the continent. A large earthquake fault may have helped the erosion.

Dr. Gary E. Parker, geology professor at San Diego's Chrisitan Heritage College, has studied the Grand Canyon both from the air and from deep within. He backpacked through the canyon with other geologists observing with special care the earthquake-faulted area of Bright Angel Creek.

And he has come to one conclusion: "Gradual erosion could never cut the pattern we see in the Grand Canyon." Parker notes that rock layers lie horizontal for over one hundred miles along the canyon's length. "This could only happen in terms of 'flood geology,'" he insists. If deposited over millions of years, he says, the pattern would be "jumbled up."

Also, he notes that the canyon's tributaries "fall off" into the canyon—evidence of sudden erosion.

But could such extensive erosion really happen in a comparatively short time?

Parker and his colleagues believe so. They point to the spectacularly deep canyons found in the hard, basaltic lava country of eastern Washington (the area resembles a miniature Grand Canyon). Most scientists accept the fact that these canyons were created by the well-documented "Great Spokane Flood" of only a few thousand years ago.

Interestingly, Grand Canyon park rangers are beginning to back off of the slow process theory and allow for a more "catastrophic" view. They now talk about several models of how the canyon might have been formed. And the canyon museum includes the description of a "flood tradition" still passed on by Indians living in the canyon.

The geologic choice seems to be either between "lots of time" or "lots of water." On your next look at the Grand Canyon, you can decide what theory you prefer.

Grand Teton Trail Trekking

The Rocky Mountain Lodge and Outfitters headquarters lies just four miles outside Grand Teton National Park, and it specializes in hosting youth groups.

If your group of Christian young people wants an adventure in Jackson, Wyoming, the hosts at Rocky Mountain Lodge (formerly workers with Youth for Christ) will make sure you get it.

If you stay for five days, they can probably take you on an overnight wilderness camp-out, guide you in white-water rafting down the Snake River, and lead you in sight-seeing tours of both the Grand Tetons and Yellowstone.

You'd probably also get a tram ride at a Teton ski village, a half-day hike into the

Tetons, and a slide down Snow King Mountain on a coaster. Then there's always the nightly campfires, swimming at the hot springs, a little horseback riding, and a Bar J Chuckwagon Supper and Western Show.

Spacious bunkhouses can handle up to thirty-five guys and twenty-six girls, with a third bunkhouse for staff and guests. Food service includes main lodge dining and all trail food or meals for day trips.

And built into all this activity will also be a strong spiritual emphasis, including regular Bible study hours and a broad choice of exciting biblical electives.

For complete information write: Rocky Mountain Ministries, Inc., Star Route Box 373, Jackson, Wyoming 83001.

Green, Keith

Christians everywhere were shocked when, on July 28, 1982, singer/songwriter Keith Green and eleven others were killed in a plane crash in Van, Texas.

Keith Green began playing a ukulele at age three, guitar at five, and piano at six. He wrote his first song at eight, recorded his first record at ten and signed his first recording contract (with Decca) at eleven.

He was born of Jewish parents, but raised in Christian Science. Though proud of his Jewish heritage, Keith searched for something more. Drugs, astrology, the occult, and obscure religions didn't satisfy him. Then at age nineteen, after a bad LSD trip, he put his faith in Jesus Christ, and his life changed overnight.

Later he married a girl, Melody, also of Jewish descent, and they became songwriters for CBS. But they left their promising careers to give their lives full-time to the Lord's work with their Last Days Ministry.

Keith Green, singing at the piano songs he had written himself, staged concerts before tens of thousands across the country, urging Christians to live completely for Jesus. His songs were saturated with Scripture. The message was serious, but also often full of humor—like his popular number, "So You Wanna Go Back to Egypt." It chides the children of Israel who grumbled and complained, even when God was blessing them every day with manna from heaven. The song suggests they enjoyed "manna hotcakes," "manna souffle," and even "bamanna bread!"

Keith Green didn't like to charge high prices for his popular record albums (he recorded five), so he would just tell kids to take them home and send him the money later—whatever they could afford. He also warned kids that they shouldn't idolize Christian rock singers, but that instead they should look to Jesus.

The life of Keith Green, even though it was cut short, spoke loudly to thousands of young people. His songs and life example continue to point many to Jesus.

Photo courtesy of Sparrow Records

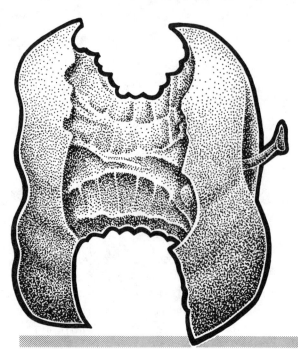

Hams

Seated by your amateur "ham" radio, you're eager for a good contact from someone out there on the shortwave frequency band assigned to "hams." You call "CQ" several times, give your call sign, and release the push-to-talk button. (The signal *CQ*, an invitation to talk, is short for *call to quarters*.)

You don't know who will answer. It could be someone only a few miles away. Or, because the signals of ham radios bounce off the ionosphere, your signal could "skip" hundreds, even thousands, of miles.

When someone answers, you can hardly wait until he identifies himself. The other ham operator could be from out of the state—or from out of the country!

Once in a while, some lucky operator gets a contact with Jordan's King Hussein. He is also an avid ham radio operator. Many hams exchange postcards with other operators they've contacted, and so build a collection of cards from around the world.

You have to be at least eighteen years of age to get a license for a C.B. (Citizens Band) short-distance radio, the kind most commonly used in cars and trucks. But there's no age limit in ham radio. So a number of kids are on the air. If you can correctly answer a fairly simple set of questions administered by a ham in your hometown, you can qualify for Novice Class privileges. Then you need to buy, remodel, or build receiving and transmitting equipment,

For the meanings of these signals, see page 224.

at a cost ranging from $50 to over $1,000.

There are some 400,000 licensed amateur radio operators in the United States, and 360,000 in other countries, many of whom speak English.

Christians with the hobby of ham radio often run across other Christians in their contacts, and some U.S. hams conduct Bible studies over the radio. Radio can also be a means of talking to someone else about the Lord.

Some ham radio hobbyists have been able to put this knowledge to work on the mission field, where telephone service is not always available. Sometimes ham radio operators can use radio to assist in emergencies.

Your radio store, library, or newsstand will carry amateur radio magazines like *QST, CQ,* and *Ham Radio.* And for information about becoming a ham, you can write to: American Radio Relay League, Newington, Connecticut 06111.

(For more on radio, see *Quito's Shortwave Superpower* and *Radio Waves.*)

Hatchets

George Washington chopped down a cherry tree with a hatchet as a boy, so the story goes, and got into trouble for it.

Carry Nation, one of American history's most unusual women, used a hatchet in another way. She chopped up taverns.

Carry Nation was furious at what she had seen strong drink, or alcohol, do to the lives of men and women. Her first husband had been one of its tragic victims.

So one day in 1900 she barged into a saloon in southern Kansas and began to smash chairs, break mirrors, and ax the furniture. At the same time she preached to the startled owner and his customers about the evils of drink. She continued her raids for several years.

Today alcohol still destroys many lives. It also causes half of the nation's fatal automobile accidents. Carry Nation was right in her concern about alcoholism. By wielding the hatchet, she called dramatic attention to this very serious problem. But most would agree that her methods were wrong.

Haystack Monument

Ripley's "Believe-It-or-Not" once called this structure "the world's only monument to a haystack." You will find it at Williamstown, in the Berkshire Mountains of northwest Massachusetts.

How did a haystack ever deserve a monument?

Actually, the monument honors five dedicated Christian college students who once took shelter under the haystack in a thunderstorm. In 1806 New England's spiritual climate had fallen to a low ebb. Anti-Christian demonstrations at Williams College had even forced new converts to form a secret society. Discouraged, one summer afternoon five Christian students met in a maple grove for private prayer. A sudden rain shower drove them to the shelter of the haystack.

There the students prayed about a plan to reach the unevangelized world with the message of Jesus Christ. When the sun broke through the clouds, the voice of Samuel J. Mills rang with confidence: "We can do it if we will." From that moment on, the students went forward with a new zeal and confidence that God was going to do something great in their lives.

And God did. From this small band of students would come some of the greatest missionaries of all time—among them Luther Rice and Adoniram Judson.

In 1980 Christian college students renewed the petition of these early Christians. Young people dedicated to the cause of world missions gathered around the Haystack Monument to pray that a revival in missions would happen in the twentieth century.

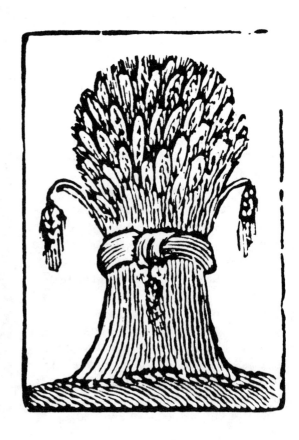

Hiding Place

Every kid has enjoyed the game of hide-and-seek. But for many Jews in Nazi-ruled Europe, hiding wasn't a game. It was a matter of life and death.

Sometimes Christians risked their own lives to shelter Jews in their town. One courageous woman named Corrie ten Boom and her family hid Jewish people from the Nazis in a secret room above the family clock shop in Holland.

For two years the family concealed a continual parade of Jewish refugees and helped them escape the country. They conducted regular drills to make sure they could hide all the Jews and every trace of their belongings within two minutes flat.

But one day the hideout was discovered. The Nazis cast the ten Booms into their infamous Ravensbruck prison camp. There Corrie and her sister Betsie tried to spread God's love amidst hate and despair.

A small Bible was smuggled into the barracks, and soon a prayer group flourished. Somehow the Nazis never discovered it.

Exhausted and ill, Betsie died in Ravensbruck. Though earmarked for execution herself, Corrie one day was singled out in the roll call and miraculously released. It surely seemed to be an answer to the prayers of those who had been with her in Barracks 28.

When Corrie ten Boom left prison, she began to help those who had gone through the same kind of tragic experience. She also struggled to learn to forgive those who had harmed her family.

Corrie's book, *The Hiding Place*, has sold millions of copies. Later the story was made into a film. And Corrie has traveled to other countries and told her story to audiences around the world.

After World War II, Corrie ten Boom received knighthood from Queen Juliana of

Betsie ten Boom cries out for her sister as they are herded on a train to a concentration camp in the film The Hiding Place.

Photo courtesy of World Wide Pictures

the Netherlands. The government of Israel honored her as a "righteous Gentile" and planted a tree in her honor. Israel has since honored others in the same way, but if you go to the grove of trees at the Yad Vashem Museum in Jerusalem today, you will find her tree marked "Number 1."

Tragically, the Nazis at Ravensbruck had designated ninety-six thousand women for death. Why was Corrie released? How did God arrange to spare her for her ministry around the world in years to come?

Years after her release, Corrie ten Boom learned why her prisoner identification number had come up for release rather than that of a more likely candidate.

The Nazis had made a clerical error.

SEND FOR: *Hiding Place* Comic Book

For information on how you may obtain the story of Corrie ten Boom and *The Hiding Place* in comic book form, see instructions under *Archie*.

High Voltage

The man removes his shoes and steps into direct contact with a transformer of one million volts. Someone pulls a switch. The million volts surge through his body and fire streaks from his fingertips. The man survives!

One million volts through the human body and still alive? Impossible!

That's what most people would think. But Dr. Irwin Moon, founder of the well-known Moody Institute of Science, has been doing it for years. So have some of his associates.

In the film *Facts of Faith*, Dr. Moon lets you see it firsthand. But he also explains.

"Ordinary house current is 60-cycle alternating current," he says. If he were to take a million volts with the frequency at 60 cycles, per second, he explains, "it would be instantly fatal."

But for his electrifying act, the frequency is raised to 65,000 cycles per second. At this higher speed, the current tends to flow on the surface of the skin, away from vital organs. It is still not an easy demonstration. Dr. Moon must wear metal caps on his fingertips to prevent serious burns and to give the high voltage an outlet.

Moon follows his first feat with another in which he holds a two-by-four plank of wood in his hands.

The switch is pulled. The electrical power sets the board on fire!

Hockey Profile

In a rough sport like ice hockey, it's easy to lose your cool.

Take the case of Dave Forbes, former National Hockey League forward, who played four seasons with the Boston Bruins. Some of you might have heard of the incident that made headlines in early 1975.

Forbes got into a fight on the rink with Henry Boucha of the Minnesota North Stars. If you've watched hockey on tv, you have probably seen many fights. But in this

case, Forbes was indicted by a grand jury for "aggravated assault with a dangerous weapon." As a result, he became the first professional athlete in the United States to be tried in a court of law for an act of aggression during an athletic contest.

It might have been a landmark case, but the ten-day trial resulted in a hung jury and the case was not retried. If convicted, Forbes would have spent three years in jail.

But that's not the end of the Dave Forbes story.

Two years later, on New Year's Eve, while most of his teammates partied,

Forbes sat in his hotel room and reviewed his life-style. Privately, he surrendered his life to Jesus Christ.

It was several months before he began to talk about what had happened, but his teammates had already noticed the difference. Forbes also met another Christian, Tom Reid of the Minnesota North Stars, who encouraged him in his new faith. (Other active Christians in hockey include Ed Kea of the Atlanta Flames and Dean Talafous of the New York Rangers.)

Forbes later decided to retire from hockey, and has spent the last two years in Bible school and seminary.

There was no chapel program among pro hockey players as there is in baseball and football until recently, when such a program was started by Hockey Ministries, International. HMI also conducts eight week-long Christian Athlete Hockey Camps in the summer for youngsters 10 to 16. For information on the camps, write to: Fellowship of Christian Athletes, 8701 Leeds Road, Kansas City, Missouri 64129.

Hunger

Remember the last time you sat down at the table at home, and told everyone, "I'm starved"? It was just an expression, of course. You felt hungry, but food wasn't very far away.

Yet for more than 225 million undernourished children in the world, the food just *isn't* there. Wars, diseases, droughts, earthquakes, hurricanes—disasters like these leave families around the world without a way to get proper nourishment.

Do you wish you could help, but don't know how?

Fortunately, a large number of Christian relief and development organizations are operating now to try to aid these people. And you can get involved.

What does "relief and development" mean? *Relief* means helping people right after a disaster, handing out emergency food and medicine. *Development* means helping people get back on their feet and care for themselves, by teaching them such skills as better farming techniques and improved medical hygiene. This saying explains development pretty well: "Give a man a fish and you feed him for a day; teach a man to fish and you feed him for a lifetime."

Many fine Christian groups work in relief and development. And several of them have specific ways that kids can get involved in helping needy people around the world.

World Vision has three programs designed for kids. The "Bite" program, for grades one through six, provides materials for Sunday school classes to study Bible passages about helping others—and also to raise money for the hungry. The "Planned Famine" program for junior high, high school, and college kids, involves thirty

After a hurricane on the Caribbean island of St. Lucia, life looks grim.

hours of fasting and learning about why hunger exists in the world and what can be done—plus raising money for the cause. The "Love Loaf" program, for the entire family, involves a little bank shaped like a loaf of bread. As you and your family pray about the needy people in the world each day, you can keep adding to the money in the bank and then donate it.

World Relief has two programs of interest to kids. "Supersweat," geared to junior high and high school students, involves Bible learning and—believe it or not—exercise! Each kid signs up sponsors to donate a certain amount of money for each sit-up, push-up, or jumping jack he or she does. The "Skip a Lunch, Feed a Bunch" program involves the whole family in skipping a meal once a week for six to eight weeks and donating the money saved to help the hungry. Bible study material and a lunch-box-shaped bank are included.

Compassion International says that for only five dollars per month, you can provide nutritious meals for an undernourished child somewhere. Compassion will send you reports about the children being helped, and also *Compassion* magazine.

We've listed the addresses of these three organizations below, plus other Christian organizations you might want to contact in order to do something about the problem of hunger. You could also ask your pastor if your church or denomination has a program to help needy people for Jesus' sake; many denominations do.

• Compassion International, P.O. Box 7000, Colorado Springs, Colorado 80933.

• Food for the Hungry, 7729 East Greenway Road, Scottsdale, Arizona 85260.

• World Concern, 19303 Fremont Avenue North, Seattle, Washington 98133.

• World Relief, P.O. Box WRC, Wheaton, Illinois 60187.

• World Vision, 919 West Huntington Drive, Monrovia, California 91016.

Hymn Records

In case you didn't know it, the name of hymn writer Fanny Crosby can be found in the *Guinness Book of World Records.* Labeled the "most prolific hymnist," she wrote more than eighty-five hundred hymns, even though she couldn't see! (Fan-ny had been blinded at the age of six weeks.) Charles Wesley, also quick with a pen, wrote about six thousand hymns.

The longest English hymn ever written was "The Sands of Time Are Sinking," which had 152 lines in its original form (most hymnbooks have trimmed it to 32 lines). The shortest hymn is "Be Present at Our Table, Lord," which is sung as grace at mealtime.

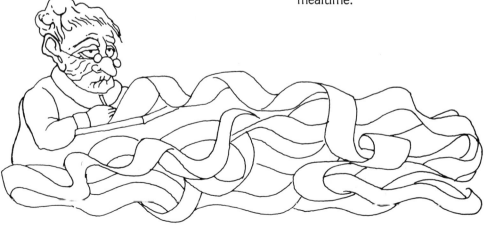

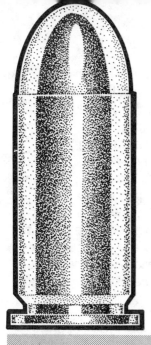

Israel

In the course of history, the world has seen the rise and fall of many nations. But only one nation has risen again after being disbanded nearly two thousand years.

It is the nation of Israel.

Old Testament prophets warned that Israel would be scattered among the people of the earth. Jesus said its people would be "led captive into all the nations" (Luke 21).

In A.D. 70, that is exactly what happened. Roman legions destroyed Israel. It was no

more. Its peoples soon dispersed among the nations of the earth.

Then in May 1948, during the time of President Truman, Israel was reestablished as an independent state. Jewish people from all over the world came back to their land.

It seems incredible that any people scattered for nearly two thousand years could retain their national identity. Logic says they should have been absorbed into other cultures centuries ago.

But that is not what the Bible said would happen. In Ezekiel 38, the prophet said that Israel would someday reassemble as a nation.

Common sense says the Jews should have totally "lost" their language. That didn't happen either. The Hebrew language has been revived. Jewish people, including children, who return to Israel today must promptly learn it. (That means everyone must learn to write from right to left!)

It was all foreseen in the Bible. And it's just one more piece of evidence that the Bible is no ordinary book.

Ivy League

Harvard. Yale. Princeton. Dartmouth. What do they have in common? They are all famous universities in New England that belong to the "Ivy League," some of the oldest and best schools in the country. The term "Ivy League" comes from the fact that the buildings of older universities are commonly covered with this climbing vine.

That may not surprise you. But most people are surprised to learn that all of these schools were founded by Christians.

Harvard is the oldest, founded by the Puritans in 1638, only eighteen years after the Pilgrims landed at Plymouth Rock. Harvard's first presidents insisted that there could be no true knowledge or wisdom without Jesus Christ. Half of its early graduates become ministers.

Christians in the Connecticut region launched Yale, also to train ministers. Princeton (originally called "The College of New Jersey") sprang up in part from the great religious revival that swept New England in the early 1700s, the First Great Awakening. Dartmouth was founded as a missionary school for reaching the Indians.

As the frontier moved west, Christians founded other schools. In fact, quite a few of today's prominent universities were started by churches—all the way west to the University of California!

Unfortunately, many of these schools eventually lost their original spiritual focus. But the spirit of Christian education goes on in the Bible institutes and the Christian colleges and universities of today.

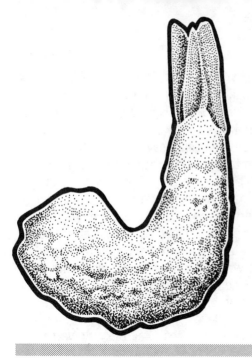

Japan Explosion

In 1942 a dentist in Japan, Dr. Yoshinori Ishihama, was sentenced to prison for holding a Christian meeting in his home. In those days the Japanese emperor was worshiped as a god, and loyalty to Jesus was seen as disloyalty to the nation's ruler.

For a while, Dr. Ishihama's fear caused him to deny his faith. But in prison he returned to his trust in God again.

Still in his prison cell in Hiroshima on August 6, 1945, Dr. Ishihama suddenly heard a tremendous explosion. The first atomic bomb had been dropped on the city by an American plane. Buildings around the prison were instantly flattened. A mile away, in the center of Hiroshima, eighty thousand people were dead or injured.

Yet in the midst of the tragedy, something miraculous had occurred. The thick prison walls had kept Dr. Ishihama from harm!

Allied troops soon set Dr. Ishihama free, and he was reunited with his family in Kobe, Japan. Because God used a prison to spare his life, he has been able to share the gospel in that city now for more than thirty-five years.

This family crest shows the Japanese national emblem, the rising sun, on a fan.

Jet Pilot

Early in 1976, the Air Force cautiously announced that it would seek ten women for jet pilot training.

Women to fly jets? Some thought it wouldn't work. Said one skeptical pilot, "A woman would not even be able to hold the brakes!"

One day seasoned jet pilot Rich Engel, noting his wife's casual interest in some of his training manuals that were lying around the house, suggested she apply.

Connie Engel, busy at work in the kitchen, thought the idea ridiculous!

But the Engels, who had recently become Christians, committed the idea to the Lord. Circumstances soon converged to suggest she should at least take the first step.

Connie took an entrance test filled with seemingly endless questions. "Have you ever jump started an automobile?" No.

"Have you ever taken a carburetor apart?" No.

"Do you have a private pilot's license?" No. . . .

She failed it—until the Air Force conceded that the exam had been designed for men, and that the women should be given another chance. Connie promptly expanded her mechanical skills, secured her private pilot's license, reapplied, and passed!

Then followed weeks—even months—of demanding aircraft academics, vigorous physical training, and many hours in the cockpit—first in a simulator, then behind the actual controls. In back of her sat the instructor, directing her moves and ready to take the controls at a split second in any emergency.

During these months the other women in the program observed Connie's coolness and her Christian faith in action. Often they came to her with problems.

It was traditional at Williams Air Force

Base in Arizona for a man who soloed successfully for the first time to be thrown in a huge water tank. When Connie and the other women took their first flights, the men added a special touch to the water tank. Bubble bath!

Grinding through the months of rigorous training, Connie might have found many reasons to quit the program. Instead, she stayed with it, and graduated first in her class of men and women.

And on November 30, 1976, when she soloed in a T-37, Connie Engel became the first woman jet pilot in the United States Air Force.

Joni

Millions of kids and adults alike have come to admire artist and speaker Joni Eareckson Tada. You may know her from her starring role in the movie *Joni*, or from her best-selling book of that same name. Or, you may have heard her in person, seen her on tv, bought one of her records, or sent a note to a friend on one of her pencil-sketched greeting cards.

Joni is quite an active young woman; yet she is paralyzed from the neck down.

She sketches beautiful drawings by holding a pen or pencil in her mouth, and with a specially equipped car she even drives on the Los Angeles freeways! She has recently married Ken Tada, a high school teacher and coach who works with the Special Olympics.

Joni was a lively, athletic, full-of-fun teenager that summer day in 1967 when she dived into the cool, shallow waters of Chesapeake Bay. In a split second she became paralyzed for life.

The first two years of rehabilitation in a hospital are now almost a blur to her. At first she wanted to die. For a long time she was angry with God for letting such a thing happen—until the Lord began to work in her life. One night when she was in great pain, a friend blurted out, "Joni, Jesus knows how you feel—you aren't the only one—he was paralyzed too." The friend explained how Jesus was in pain on the cross, held immobile by the nails. This comforted Joni. She began to realize God still loved her, and that with his help her life could be full.

Joni climbed the long road back to this "full life," and learned to sketch with her teeth. Her artwork was shown on the "Today Show," and she was interviewed by Barbara Walters. That exposure caught the attention of a major Christian publisher, and the book that resulted has sold millions of copies.

When the president of Worldwide Pictures phoned Joni at her Maryland ranch home with the idea that she play herself in the film *Joni,* she couldn't believe he was serious.

"Have you guys gone bananas?" she screamed into the phone. "There's no way I can do it. For one thing, I am not an actress, and for another I don't know if I can live through it again."

But she finally agreed to go to Los Angeles for a screen test. When the director saw the footage from the test, he knew he had found his leading lady.

A double, of course, had to reenact her jackknife dive from a raft into Chesapeake Bay. But when the camera zooms in on a still form floating facedown upon the surface of the water, it is really Joni. "Though the film crew worked quickly," said an article in the *Saturday Evening Post,* "her body temperature dropped drastically during that short time in the chilly Pacific Ocean" (the Chesapeake Bay scene was filmed at California's Newport Beach). Though she was quickly wrapped in blankets, it took five hours for her body temperature to return to normal.

It was not easy for Joni to relive the emotional trauma of her own story, but she did it because she sensed God truly wanted to use the film to touch the lives of thousands who would see it.

The film and her book are now reaching out into other countries, and so is Joni personally.

When capacity crowds turned out to hear her in Bucharest, Romania, behind the Iron Curtain, she talked about freedom: that although her body could not move, her spirit was free in Christ.

Joni also spends much time with an organization she started, Joni and Friends, which is a ministry to the disabled.

To an interviewer, Joni talked about her cherished hope: "The Bible speaks of our bodies being 'glorified' in heaven. . . . I know the meaning of that now. It's the time, after my death here, when I'll be on my feet dancing."

Today Joni works with other disabled persons.

Juggling Clown

Ever try to juggle? Almost everyone does at some time or another, if only with the oranges he may have just found sitting on the kitchen counter top.

It's really not that difficult to do, says Brian Martin, a juggling clown from Gettysburg College in Pennsylvania. He can teach most people to juggle in half an hour or less. "If you practice over a bed," he suggests, "you don't have to chase the stuff you drop."

Brian Martin first learned juggling in high school, from another fellow in his church youth group. Before long, five boys from the group were juggling regularly for church programs, birthday parties, and school shows.

They got so good at it, in fact, that they performed at the Barnum Festival Ringmaster's Road Show, part of the P. T. Barnum Festival held annually near Brian's hometown in Connecticut.

In college, Brian learned to put some Christian "patter" with his act. ("Patter" is the story line that sometimes goes along with juggling.) He writes his own patters, and has done one for children's groups called "Noah and the Rainbow."

His role as a clown fits nicely with his juggling. "I like to think the symbol of the clown is an example of what Paul meant when he wrote about being 'fools for Christ's sake,'" he says. When Brian finishes college, in fact, he thinks he may join a Christian circus ministry, such as "Circus Allelujah," an eighteen-act show that travels the country.

For a catalog of unusual drama ideas you can use, see *Play by Play.*

Brian also incorporates a unicycle in his act.

Jungle Pilots

In years past it used to take missionaries days—even weeks—to reach their outposts in the interiors of Africa, South America, or the uncharted South Pacific islands.

But these days dedicated Christian "jungle pilots" fly into these remote areas around the globe, transporting missionaries, food, and medical supplies.

America supplies the majority of these fliers. So how do you get to be a jungle pilot?

The biggest percentage are trained by the flight school of the Chicago-based Moody Bible Institute. The flight school is located in Elizabethton, Tennessee, at the foot of the Appalachian Mountains.

There missionary aviation students not only learn to fly in the nearby rugged terrain; they also must know how to do all their own maintenance and, if necessary, even take the plane apart! (Out in the jungles you can't rely on finding a nearby mechanic.)

There are other Christian schools that also train pilots, located in such places as Longview, Texas, and Grand Rapids, Michigan. The Jungle Aviation and Radio Service (JAARS), an arm of the Wycliffe Bible Translators, has its U.S. base in Waxhaw, North Carolina.

And if you live in the Los Angeles area, you are not far from the Missionary Aviation Fellowhip (MAF), an air support agency that has its headquarters at Redlands Municipal Airport, southeast of San Bernardino. The facilities of MAF predominate at the airport, and someone will be pleased to take you on a tour.

If you visit on a weekday, you can probably see airplanes being readied for mission service all over the world. The shop is reported to be one of the best in aviation, and from this base missionary pilots receive advance training in the nearby mountains and deserts.

(If you want to learn more about these flying missionaries, read *Jungle Pilot* by Russ Hitt.)

Illustration by Kurt Mitchell

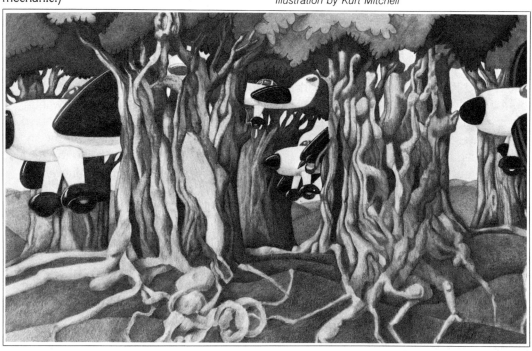

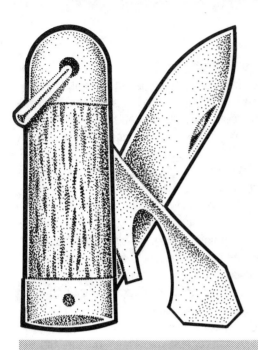

Kentucky Colonel

The smiling face of Colonel Sanders has become as familiar as the red-and-white striped buckets of his Kentucky Fried Chicken. Unlike Betty Crocker, the Chiquita Banana, or the Jolly Green Giant, all of whom are figments of someone's imagination, Colonel Harland Sanders was a real person.

When he died in 1980 at the age of ninety, he had helped to transform the food industry in North America. "Finger-lickin' good Kentucky Fried Chicken," made from the colonel's secret recipe of eleven herbs and spices, is now sold in over five thousand restaurants in North America, plus thirteen hundred more overseas.

The Kentucky colonel (an honorary title) didn't start his fried chicken chain until he was sixty-five, the age most people retire. The American operation sold in 1971 for $273 million. All the profits of his Canadian operation go to charity—about $1 million a year—including Christian causes.

Although Colonel Sanders had always been generous with his money, it was not until late in life that he became a Christian. In fact, he was seventy-nine!

Before the evangelistic service that life-changing evening in 1969, the pastor had asked the white-haired, goateed colonel to sit with him on the platform for the early part of the service.

"Oh, no," said the colonel, "I can't do that."

"You might as well," said the pastor. "Everybody will be lookin' at you. And if you sit up there, they can all see you. We'll take a seat down in front when the evangelist starts."

At the close of the sermon that night, Colonel Sanders raised his hand during the invitation, then went up to kneel at the altar. "That was what I had been wantin' all my life." he said later. "It just seemed like a great burden was lifted off my shoulders. I'd never felt anything like that before, and here I was, seventy-nine years old!"

Colonel Sanders had the opportunity late in life to let Jesus turn his life around. And he didn't chicken out!

King of the Cowboys

For years tv star Roy Rogers, known as "King of the Cowboys," and his wife, Dale Evans, have included Christian songs in their performances and talked openly of their Christian faith.

But their act wasn't always allowed to be that way. In 1952 the management of Madison Square Garden was horrified when Roy wanted to sing a religious number during their engagement there. They pleaded for him not to, and said it would be sure "professional suicide."

But Roy did it anyway. Houselights darkened. Spotlights formed the shape of a cross while Roy sang "Peace in the Valley." The applause that followed was deafening. During their forty-three performances at Madison Square Garden, the box office broke all attendance records! Though their tv show is off the air, the couple still appears on tv specials.

If your family is ever passing through California's Mojave Desert, you can visit the Roy Rogers/Dale Evans Museum at Victorville (Interstate 15), not far from their Apple Valley ranch.

Among the items on display there are Roy's famous tv horse, Trigger (in stuffed form), the saddle Roy rode in the Rose Parade, his gun collection, and a fine display of scale model western vehicles. The museum gift shop sells a full selection of the numerous Christian books Dale has written.

Ghost Town shows the park's Western motif.▶

Knott's Berry Farm

When Walter Knott and his wife, Cordelia, bought their farm near Los Angeles many years ago, building a world-famous amusement park was not on their minds!

But their ten acres of fertile land soon yielded more than enough juicy berries to sell from their tiny roadside stand. Soon, Mr. Knott helped develop the boysenberry (a crossbreed of the blackberry, loganberry, and red raspberry), which he named after its inventor—his neighbor, Rudolph Boysen.

Then the Great Depression hit—a time when most people had very little money. Cordelia Knott decided to turn her dining room into a restaurant for extra income. She served delicious fried chicken, and soon attracted crowds. In the next months, Walter Knott began to worry about how to entertain the long lineups of hungry diners waiting for their meals.

So in the early 1940s he began to assemble what would later become the nation's first theme amusement park—years before Walt Disney created Disneyland. Today Knott's Berry Farm is best known for its unique "Old West" rides and entertainment, although the park restaurant still serves tasty fried chicken to some of the four million people who visit the farm every year.

From the outset Walter and Cordelia Knott, devout Christians, determined that no liquor or strong drink would be served on their premises. The policy still stands, and it probably helped set the standard for the other family amusement parks—like Disneyland—that emerged later.

Lady Be Good's Last Flight

It was one of the great air mysteries of World War II: the strange disappearance of the *Lady Be Good.*

The plane vanished on return from its first combat mission over Naples, Italy. It was to have landed at Benghazi, Libya, on the coast of North Africa. But it never made it.

For seventeen years it was assumed that the plane ran out of fuel somewhere over the Mediterranean.

Then, like a ghost out of the past, the wreckage was finally discovered—deep in the heart of the Libyan desert. Though its crew had reported the plane "low on fuel," it had traveled nearly five hundred miles beyond its destination!

Why? And since no bodies were aboard the plane, what had happened to the crew? Men from the Moody Institute of Science flew into the desert to piece the mystery together. The result was an intriguing film called *Signposts Aloft.*

The crew, it seems, had barely settled down for the long trip home from Naples when their ADF (automatic direction finder) needle swung around in the opposite direction. It told them they had just passed their base!

Why, they weren't due home for hours, the crew reasoned. Their instruments must be damaged.

So the pilot descended beneath the clouds. They would ignore the instrument and eventually try to spot the beacon light at Benghazi.

They did not know it was already miles behind them. Nor did they realize that an unusually high tail wind had sent them whizzing past their base hours ahead of schedule.

The crew bailed out just before the crash when the plane ran out of fuel. One man's chute didn't open. He may have been the luckiest. Daytime temperatures in this region were around 140 degrees.

It was said that no man could possibly walk more than fifty miles in such heat. Yet five bodies were finally discovered—an incredible seventy-eight miles from the bailout point. And one man had walked even further: 114 miles!

Here was a classic case where the crew refused to believe their guiding instruments, and chose instead to rely upon their own logic. The film then draws a parallel from the Bible: "There is a way which seemeth right unto a man, but the end thereof are the ways of death" (Proverbs 14:12).

The film Signposts Aloft *shows the actual wreckage of the* Lady Be Good, *and attempts to solve her mystery.*

Landry, Tom

Tom Landry, coach of football's formidable Dallas Cowboys, has become a legend in his own time. He is the only coach, in fact, that the Cowboys have ever had, and he's taken them to five Super Bowls. (They've won two.)

Even before the era of the Cowboys, Landry was a success in football. He starred with the University of Texas, played in bowl games, coached with the 1956 championship New York Giants.

One day, when Landry was back home in Dallas, a friend invited him to a Bible discussion group over at a hotel. A regular churchgoer, Landry was happy to go. There for the first time he discovered the difference between being simply a churchgoer and a true Christian. That was at age thirty-three, and Landry has never been the same since.

Landry enjoys his life as a Christian and a coach. Why then, some wonder, doesn't he smile more at a game?

"The only way I can be successful is if I concentrate," says Landry. "I very seldom look at the play; I'm looking at the defense. So when they put the camera on me, I haven't seen what the fans have seen. People get that picture of me. My image hasn't changed for twenty years. I don't expect it to now."

Frank Luksa, a Dallas sportswriter who has covered the Cowboys since 1962, says Landry *does* smile. "Odds are that he won't throw a pie at Howard Cosell, but the guy does have a sense of humor."

Landry's favorite Bible verse is Philippians 4:13: "I can do all things through Christ which strengtheneth me."

"Each time I feel doubts about my ability to accomplish something," Landry says, "I always remember this verse."

SEND FOR: Landry Comic Book

For information on how you may obtain the story of "Tom Landry and the Dallas Cowboys" in comic book form, see instructions under *Archie.*

Largest Cathedral

The world's largest cathedral, affirms the *Guinness Book of World Records,* is the cathedral of St. John the Divine in New York City, which has a floor area of 121,000 square feet (larger than two football fields) and is over fifteen stories tall. Its cornerstone was laid in 1892, but the Gothic building is still under construction today. New Yorkers often refer to it as "St. John the Unfinished"!

The cathedral's architecture, stained glass, and stone carving are exceptional, and on its premises are a museum of religious art, a biblical garden, and thirteen acres of grounds. Well-known author and Christian Madeleine L'Engle often works in the library there.

Largest Congregation

Where is the largest church congregation in the world? It must be in the United States, right?

Wrong.

You will find it in Seoul, Korea.

In 1982 that city's Full Gospel Central Church had about 250,000 members! The second largest church in Seoul has sixty thousand.

By contrast, the largest churches in the United States have about twelve to fifteen thousand members.

By 1984 the Seoul Church expects to have a membership of one-half million!

Largest Sing-alongs

The world's largest all-night gospel sing-along is the Sundown to Sunup Gospel Sing, held every Fourth of July at Bonifay in the Florida panhandle.

The festival has drawn as many as thirty-three thousand people. Families bring their own folding chairs, cots, quilts, sleeping bags, blankets, and pillows. The little kids get sleepy and many adults also nap during the night. But the singing goes on.

The annual "Singing on the Mountain Gospel Festival," high up in the mountains of North Carolina, also draws a big crowd. This sing-along on the side of majestic Grandfather Mountain on the fourth Sunday of June has been a tradition for more than half a century.

On its fiftieth anniversary in 1974, fifty thousand people showed up to see Bob Hope and Johnny Cash lead the lineup of featured guests. Billy Graham also drew fifty thousand there in 1976.

Largest Student Conference

Would you believe that the largest student conference in the world has to do with missions? That thousands of college students give up a week of their Christmas vacations just to explore whether or not they should become missionaries?

That's right. And the crowd of registrants has run as high as seventeen thousand!

To house these folks, the campus movement called Inter-Varsity Christian Fellowship, which sponsors the event every three years, rents the entire campus of the University of Illinois (Champaign-Urbana). They rent all the dormitories and cafeterias, and the huge assembly hall. (Since the conference is always between Christmas and New Year's Day, most Illini students have left campus for the holidays.) The next conference is scheduled for December 1984.

And what state sends the most delegates? California, which usually sees more than two thousand young Christians fly to snowy Illinois to hear the outstanding speakers and meet with mission representatives. In the West, one airline considers the event "a major airlift."

Thousands of students gather in the assembly hall.

Photo courtesy of Dave Singer

Largest Sunday School

If you are traveling anywhere within fifty miles of Hammond, Indiana, on a Sunday in the morning or early afternoon, it's likely you'll spot a parade of buses on the highway.

They'll probably all be headed to—or from—the First Baptist Church of Hammond, Indiana, which bills itself as "the world's largest Sunday school."

On special occasions its Sunday school attendance has exceeded ten thousand people, with buses coming and going in "waves"from early morning to midafternoon!

Lawyers:Leon Jaworski

What is your image of lawyers? Many people think lawyers are dishonest, and are just out to "charge a big fee." A 1973 Harris Poll found that only eighteen percent of the public had confidence in lawyers—a rating lower than they gave to garbage collectors! Not many people would see law as a field for Christian kids to aspire to.

But the other side of this story is seen in the legal career of Leon Jaworski. Most Americans know him as the special Watergate prosecutor who doggedly sought pres-

Not all Americans realize that Jaworski's entire life was dedicated to a quiet but insistent search for truth and justice.

When Leon Jaworski was born in 1905, his father named him after Leonidas of Sparta, a Greek who gave his life for what he believed in. Jaworski's father, an evangelical pastor, challenged Leon to follow in his namesake's footsteps. "Courage in life is so very important. . . . Courage to do right and to stand up for what is right."

Jaworski remembered those words many times during his life. One difficult period was the time that he was asked to help prosecute Governor Ross Barnett of Mississippi. The governor had stopped young

idential tapes that would reveal that President Richard Nixon had committed two serious felonies (criminal offenses).

Because of the facts revealed by Jaworski and his staff, the United States Supreme Court finally ruled that these tapes (in which President Nixon was heard plotting a cover-up of White House involvement in the illegal break-in at the Democratic headquarters) would have to be given to the district court. It was this decision that ultimately did Nixon in.

Jaworski was special Watergate prosecutor.

James Meredith from entering the University of Mississippi because Meredith was black—despite two court orders.

Jaworski knew that many of his associates in his hometown of Houston, Texas, were sympathetic to Barnett's attempt to preserve segregation in the South. Yet he agreed to represent the United States government as prosecutor.

In the next months, anonymous telephone callers spewed out hateful threats when the Jaworskis answered their phone at home. Lawyers wrote letters asking Leon to resign as president of the Texas Bar Association. Threats against Jaworski became so vocal that the Houston police were assigned to protect his home.

Still Jaworski steadfastly began the proceedings to prosecute Barnett. Two years later, the charges against the governor were dismissed, because "Ole Miss" had become an integrated campus during that time—open to all American citizens: black and white.

Jaworski, who died in December 1982, saw life as a journey with many "crossroads": times when he made conscious decisions to serve the Lord by demanding truth and justice. To Leon Jaworski, there was not a better way to do this than by being a lawyer.

He'd be glad to know that more Christian young people than ever are showing an interest in law careers. One Christian school, Oral Roberts University, even has a law school accredited by the American Bar Association.

(For more about Christian lawyers and a case that may affect you, see *Bill of Rights.* For more about Leon Jaworski's life and his involvement in other historic events such as the Nazi War Crimes trials, read *Crossroads,* from David C. Cook.)

Liberty Bell Secret

The words from the Bible inscribed on the Liberty Bell read, "Proclaim Liberty throughout all the Land unto all the inhabitants Thereof." They seem appropriate for this symbol of the American Revolution. But it was only by coincidence that these words from Leviticus turned out to be so relevant.

The 2,000-lb. bell was cast in London in 1752 for the Pennsylvania statehouse while America was still under British rule. Little did the British realize at the time that it would eventually signal in the American Revolution when it rang to announce the adoption of the Declaration of Independence on July 8, 1776.

SEND FOR: Declaration of Independence

Obtain an authentic replica of the Declaration of Independence, on antique parchment, with all the signatures. Other historical documents included. (See the article on *Columbus* for information.)

Lincoln Look-alike

People magazine called him "a dead ringer for Abe Lincoln."

"People take one look at him," it reported, "and gasp in mock horror, 'Hey, I thought you were dead!'"

It happens constantly to the Rev. Bruce Hanks, especially when he dresses up in black frock coat, black bow tie, and stovepipe hat.

He is tall, spare, a little gangling. His facial features are like Lincoln's, as is his hairstyle and his beard.

He is the same size as Lincoln (6'4", 190 lbs.), and he even has a wart on his cheek where our sixteenth president had his.

But that isn't all. He is actually a distant cousin of Nancy Hanks, Lincoln's mother!

Rev. Hanks is a Baptist pastor in Minnesota. But during the bicentennial year, and the years around it, Hanks took a leave of absence from the pulpit to make the rounds of schools, churches, and civic and farm organizations throughout the U.S. He spent two summers in New Salem, Illinois, where Lincoln once lived, and put on six performances each day at the state park there.

Though back in the pulpit now, Hanks still travels some. Usually he delivers a slide lecture about Lincoln's life and then gives the Gettysburg Address.

Students rarely forget the day "Abraham Lincoln" comes to their school.

The two questions they ask most are, "Are you really a relative of Abraham Lincoln?" and "Is that a real beard?"

To both questions his answer is "yes."

There's one more coincidence. Lincoln's wife's name was Mary Ann Todd. Bruce Hanks's wife's name is also Mary Ann!

SEND FOR: Gettysburg Address

Obtain an authentic replica of Lincoln's Gettysburg Address, on antique parchment in his handwriting and with his signature. Other historical documents included. (See *Columbus*.)

Lost Ark

The recent movie hit *Raiders of the Lost Ark* called the nation's attention to ancient Israel's Ark of the Covenant. This sacred, gold-covered chest contained the broken tablets of the original Ten Commandments that Moses carried down from Mt. Sinai. The people of Israel sometimes carried the Ark with them into battle to protect them, because it was a symbol of God's presence.

In *Raiders of the Lost Ark*, swashbuckling archaeologist Indiana Jones, escaping death at almost every turn, uncovers the Ark at an archaeological dig in the desert outside of Cairo, Egypt. But the Nazis also are in hot pursuit of the Ark, eager to

The Meyerses pose in costumes for People Weekly.

Photo by Jack Vartoogian/PEOPLE WEEKLY, © 1981 Time, Inc.

claim this supposedly powerful treasure for Adolf Hitler.

Of course, Christians know that the Ark itself had no power aside from what God gave it. And while the movie plot makes for great adventure, few find any evidence, biblical or otherwise, that the Ark ever found its way into Egypt.

Meanwhile, at the same time *Raiders of the Lost Ark* was showing at movie theaters across the U.S., American archaeologists Eric and Carol Meyers were at their usual work in Galilee, Israel. In their excavations in the summer of 1981, they uncovered the remains of a synagogue ark dating from 300 A.D.. This sort of ark was used in synagogues to hold the scrolls of the Torah.

Though the Meyerses had found an excellent specimen of an ark, they hadn't found the one and only Ark of the Covenant. Yet because of the popularity of *Raiders*, the husband-and-wife archaeological team found themselves instantly famous. *People* magazine even ran an article on them, and had them dress up like Indiana Jones and his girl friend Marian for the occasion (see photo).

The Meyerses didn't like *Raiders'* portrayal of archaeology as a greedy treasure hunt. Says Eric, "The real beauty of a dig is that you never know what you are going to find." They did find danger as well as ancient artifacts on their dig: scorpions, pit vipers, and unexploded bombs from Israel's war of independence!

Meanwhile, what really happened to the Ark of the Covenant? Is it still in existence somewhere? And if so, where? Theories on where the Ark might be hidden abound. Here are a few:

1. It was carted away to Ethiopia, some speculate, by Menelik, the son of King Solomon and the Queen of Sheba. (History establishes that a Jewish remnant did flee to Ethiopia.)

2. It is still hidden in one of the many subterranean caverns underneath the city of Jerusalem. It was stored away there, some say, to save it from capture by the Babylonians when they invaded Jerusalem.

3. Another theory says it was hauled off to Babylon (in what is now Iraq), and still remains there somewhere underneath that city's restored ruins.

4. In the most startling story of all, a search party headed by Tom Crotser of Winfield, Kansas, says it already found the Ark in 1981 in a cavern under Jordan's Mt. Pisgah. But the Jordanian government, says Crotser, will not let his party reenter the site. Most reputable archaeologists dismiss Crotser's story as a hoax.

5. From the scientific point of view, most archaeologists lean more toward the theory that the Ark may be buried about twenty miles outside Jerusalem at Engedi, in the cave where David hid from Saul. In 1977 American geologists, using instruments, detected a cavern there, with its entrance walled in by stone. But Israeli authorities will not permit excavation.

Other stories point to the ancient Jewish fortress of Masada, and even to Rome (one report says it is stored in a cave under a monastery there).

Only time will reveal if any of these theories are really true. Meanwhile, you can read more about it in Doug Wead's paperback book, *Where Is the Lost Ark?*

Love

The U.S. Postal Service released the stamp shown here in 1979. It turned out to be the most popular stamp it has ever issued.

Probably some buyers were purchasing the stamps for letters to their boyfriends or girl friends. The Postal Service may have sensed this when it released in 1982 another stamp with the theme of love—this one even better suited for love notes.

Love is always a popular theme. The most famous verse in the Bible speaks of love. "For God so loved the world . . ."

That's where all real love starts. With God. The Bible says that we can love him because he first loved us (I John 4: 19).

And once we truly discover how to love the Lord, we find it easier to love other people.

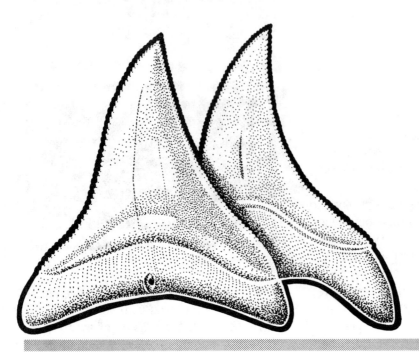

Magazines

Like to read? Then one of these Christian magazines might just be geared to your needs and interests.

Athletes in Action. A quarterly Christian

sports magazine, with stories and sports news, which can be found in most larger Christian bookstores at $2.25 a copy. (Not available by subscription.) Produced by Here's Life Publishers, a part of Campus Crusade for Christ.

Campus Life. A monthly magazine popular among high schoolers, affiliated with Youth for Christ. Emphasis on the balanced Christian life, with true stories, fiction, humor, popular columns, and excellent photography. Subscription price $14.95 a year. Write: *Campus Life,* 465 E. Gundersen Dr., Carol Stream, Illinois 60187.

Christian Athlete. A magazine for youth published bimonthly (every other month) by the Fellowship of Christian Athletes. Features personal stories by athletes, plus articles on sports and the Christian life. Subscription price $8.00 per year. Write: *The Christian Athlete,* 8701 Leeds Road, Kansas City, Missouri 64129.

Dash. A magazine for boys eight to eleven. Includes adventure stories, hobby stories, science, outdoor life, Christian boys in action. Published eight times a year by Christian Service Brigade (see article). Subscription $8.00 a year. Write: *Dash,* P.O. Box 150, Wheaton, Illinois 60187.

Telling the Truth. A Christian photojournalism and feature magazine. Offers practical help on problems young people face, plus interviews with noted Christians and news reports on youth in action. Six issues for $5.00 ($6.00 in Canada). Write *Telling the Truth,* 12814 U.S. 41 North, Evansville, Indiana 47711.

Trails. A bimonthly magazine for boys and girls in first through sixth grades, filled with stories and activities. Published by Pioneer Ministries, Inc. Subscription $3.00 a year for Pioneer Club members, $5.00 a year for nonmembers. Write: *Trails,* P.O. Box 788, Wheaton, Illinois 60187. (See also *Pioneer Clubs.*)

Venture. A magazine for young men aged twelve to eighteen, with stories and articles on topics of interest. Published eight times a year by Christian Service Brigade (see article). Subscription $6.00 a year. Write: *Venture,* P.O. Box 150, Wheaton, Illinois 60187.

Young Ambassador. A monthly magazine especially geared to young teens. Fiction stories, sports profiles, science, humor, news of things Christian teens are doing. Published by the Back to the Bible Broadcast. Subscription $9.00 a year. Write: *Young Ambassador,* P.O. Box 82808, Lincoln, Nebraska 68501.

Majorette Champ

Who is the girl below? She is Heather Dawne Smith, baton twirling champion,

who in 1982 won the Junior Miss Majorette of America title—for the second time.

Heather entered her first baton twirling contest when she was only fourteen months old! She has been twirling ever since. She won the Missouri state twirling title as a tiny tot, juvenile, preteen, and junior. During her career the 5'2" girl has won some six hundred trophies!

Heather doesn't just twirl the baton. She also plays the violin in an all-district symphony orchestra, acts in plays, sings in musicals, dances tap and ballet, models, and does an occasional television commercial. She is an honor student at Pattonville High School, near St. Louis, where she has already been inducted into her school's "hall of fame."

And she is also a regular in the cast of the St. Louis-based Super Gang, a talented Christian group which performs in rallies and on television (see *Super Gang*).

"Without Jesus, none of my activities would be worthwhile," Heather says. Although she's used to competition, Heather notes that she felt "butterflies" when competing for the 1982 national majorette title. Then she adds, "I realized that God had never left me alone before . . . and, praise to God, I won the title."

Mandrell, Barbara

Barbara Mandrell's career as a singer, like that of many others in country music, began in the choir loft of a small church.

Her dad owned a music store, and by the time she was eleven, she had learned to play several instruments, including the banjo, steel and bass guitars, and saxophone.

The woman who has won two back-to-back Entertainer of the Year awards from the Country Music Association says, "It's an asset to be a Christian in show business," and says she often "turns to the Lord for strength."

It's also not easy, of course, to maintain high moral standards in her kind of work—which includes the kinds of songs a show's producer may want his celebrity to sing, and the kind of clothing he may want her to wear. Barbara often refuses to sing a song she does not think is proper. And, at her insistence, her show always closes with a four- or five-song medley of gospel music. In 1982 she also released her first gospel album, which won a Grammy award.

Photo courtesy of Sparrow Records

Mastodon

Have you ever dug a hole in your backyard and found something unusual?

When construction workers were digging the bed of an artificial lake on the property of Judge Joseph Perry in Glen Ellyn, Illinois, their shovels struck something hard. It was a large bone.

When taken to nearby Wheaton College for examination, the bone turned out to be that of an American mastodon, dead thousands of years!

Soon geology students and professors from the college worked to excavate the rest of the animal's bones. The skeleton was then reconstructed and put on display,

with a part of the skin and hair reproduced to show what the animal would have looked like when alive.

The Perry Mastodon stands 9½ feet tall, has tusks 8½ feet long, and probably weighed ten thousand to twelve thousand pounds. Fortunately he was a vegetarian!

If you go to the mastodon display at Wheaton College, a tape will tell you the whole story. But if you happen to be there on April Fools' Day, you may hear a different tape. This one, created by some students as a prank, claims that "Perry the Mastodon" is still alive, and is fed steaks and chocolate chip cookies daily by his friends!

Memory Expert

The name of Jerry Lucas—an All-American and an Olympic Gold Medal Winner—is already down in the record books as one of the all-time basketball greats.

Then Lucas became a nationally known memory expert with his best-seller, *The Memory Book.* Appearing on Johnny Carson's "Tonight Show," he memorized the names of more than two hundred members of the audience as they stood in line at NBC, and was prepared to recite the contents of the latest *Time* magazine!

Then one weekend in 1974, in a California church, Jerry Lucas became a Christian. His wife Sharalee, already a believer, was elated. She promptly encouraged her husband to pursue a study of the New Testament.

This soon inspired Lucas to develop a chapter-by-chapter system for helping Christians to memorize the whole Bible, beginning with the New Testament.

And so Lucas wrote another book, entitled *Remember the Word.* It is impossible to explain his method in these pages, but it works. He can take a stranger and teach him all of Matthew 7 in five to seven minutes!

Because Jerry Lucas knows the power of the Bible in the hearts of men, he has conducted many seminars to help people apply his memory techniques to the Bible.

"I love the Word of God," he says, "and I'm fortified daily by having it stored in my heart."

Microphones

Any good public speaker or singer today knows how to use a microphone. (Some almost swallow it!) We take such amplification devices for granted today, but speakers and singers of earlier generations simply had to use their natural voices.

Evangelist George Whitefield of England had such a powerful voice that he could speak outdoors to a crowd of twenty thousand people, and everyone could hear him!

When George Whitefield came to Philadelphia, however, one of his admirers, Benjamin Franklin, decided he needed a good building for his evangelism. So Franklin helped raise the funds for a structure that would accommodate the crowds wanting to hear Whitefield preach. The structure they built became the first building of what is now the University of Pennsylvania.

And that is why George Whitefield's statue stands today on this state university campus.

Mile Runner

Who is the most famous American miler? A young man named Jim Ryun.

In 1964 Ryun became the first high school student to run the mile in less than four minutes. And he was only a junior! Then in 1967 he set a world record for the mile at 3:51.1 minutes, which stood for eight years.

At the Olympics in Munich in 1972, Ryun was fouled during the qualifying heats and fell. That and other injuries eventually moved Ryun to retire from competition.

Just five months before that fall, Ryun had accepted Christ as his Savior. His advice to young athletes today is that it's important to make Jesus your Lord from the very beginning of your athletic career. Only this, Ryun believes, will give you "the greatest satisfaction."

The first world record for the mile, by the way, was posted in 1864 by Charles Lawes of Britain. His time was 4:56, more than a minute slower than Ryun's a century later. Roger Bannister of Britain broke the four-minute barrier in 1954 by running the mile in 3:59.4. As of this writing the record is held by another Britisher, Sebastian Coe, who in August 1981 posted a time of 3:47.33 for the outdoor mile.

Mixed-up Mail

When little kids write to someone famous, they don't always get the address quite right.

Billy Graham, for instance, tells his listeners on radio and tv, "Just write to me: Billy Graham, Minneapolis, Minnesota." But little ears sometimes hear it another way. Here are some examples of mail he has received from kids.

Billy Graham
Many Happyness
Many Soda, USA

Billy Graham
Many Apples and
Many Soilder

Or, try this one:

Billy Graham
Many Applause,
Many Sorrow.

If you don't believe it, just visit the Billy Graham Center Museum on the campus of Wheaton College near Chicago, Illinois. Copies of all three of these letters are posted there in an exhibit.

Moby Dick

On Johnny Cake Hill in New Bedford, Massachusetts, stands a church with a pulpit shaped like the bow of a ship!

It's the church that Herman Melville, author of the great children's classic, *Moby Dick*, used to attend as a child. It's also a church designed especially for the seamen and fishermen who anchor nearby.

Much of what Melville describes in the seventh and eighth chapters of his book comes from his childhood images of this church. The church has marked the pew where Melville used to sit as an eight-year-old.

Model Kids

Meet Rick Whitmer, age fourteen, and his brother Steve, twelve. Nobody can say they haven't been "model kids" right from the start.

That's because, you see, they have both been professional models since they were babies. Rick calls it "hard work" but "fun," and he says the money is worth it. The brothers take an average of two hour-long jobs each week.

Rick says he most enjoyed filming a commercial on board a riverboat. Steve remembers the day he posed with two players of the Chicago Sting soccer team.

It's not always easy to stand still or create poses, and you've got to be able to flash a relaxed smile. But Rick and Steve would come by it naturally, if anyone would. Their father, Jim Whitmer, is a professional photographer whose work has appeared in many publications, both Christian and secular. Their mother is a model!

Rick, 14, displays his photogenic talent.

Photo courtesy of Jim Whitmer

Monkey Business

In March 1981, thirteen-year-old Kasey Segraves went on the witness stand in a Sacramento, California courtroom.

Why? It all started when Kasey's father, Kelly Segraves, grew concerned because the California schools were teaching that evolution accounted for the origin of the world's life. They were teaching it as a fact. And they were not mentioning the idea of creation at all. Mr. Segraves decided to file a suit against the state board of education.

When Kasey appeared on the witness stand, he testified that his sixth-grade teacher had told him, contrary to his religious beliefs, that man evolved from apes. The teacher did not convince him, Kasey said, nor did it shake his faith. But he

wanted the California schools to teach evolution as just a theory.

The judge ruled in the Segraveses' favor, and reaffirmed a 1973 California policy that evolution not be taught as dogma.

Interestingly, before the famous Scopes "Monkey Trial" of 1927, most public schools taught that God had created man and the universe. John Scopes wanted to teach Darwin's theory of evolution in school—and got fired when he did. Said his defense lawyer, Clarence Darrow, "It was bigotry for public schools to teach only one theory of origins."

Darrow's client won his case. But guess what? Now most public schools teach only one theory of origins: evolution!

Many Christians are arguing that both views should be taught in the classroom, and that kids ought to make up their own minds, based on scientific evidence. Where public schools have tried it, they say, the kids learn science better.

Some states now have statutes promoting balanced treatments of different views about what happened at the beginning of the universe. Others, like California, are at least making teachers admit that evolution is just a theory, not a fact.

That's why it's important that Christians—even Christian kids—stand up for their rights. (See *Bill of Rights*.)

Moody, Dwight

Much of the world today knows the name of evangelist Billy Graham. But one hundred years ago, the evangelist they knew was Dwight L. Moody.

A shoe salesman in Boston led young Moody to the Lord. He came to Chicago, and turned his energies to a Sunday school he had started among the poor kids on Chicago's near north side.

The class met first in an old dance hall, then later in an abandoned freight car! Moody would ride a pony to round up his kids, handing out a supply of maple sugar and apples to encourage them.

The class grew into the hundreds. It drew such attention that once President Abraham Lincoln visited it.

Later Moody conducted great evangelistic crusades across America and in Great Britain. Over the years he spoke to many millions. In 1886 he founded Chicago's Moody Bible Institute. He died in Kansas City in 1899.

Interestingly, Moody also had a ship named in his honor (see photo). The S.S. *Dwight L. Moody* was launched in June 1943, and transported military and commercial cargo in the European, African, and Pacific war theaters in World War II.

After that war, it sat in the national defense reserve fleet at Beaumont, Texas. Only a few years ago it was scrapped—and sent to a ship's graveyard.

Moon Facts

For centuries people on earth looked at "the man in the moon." In this century we've put men *on* the moon (see *Astronaut*). And from this close-up look at our nearest neighbor in space, we've learned some interesting facts.

Scientists were pretty surprised by some of them.

Most of the scientific establishment would put the age of the moon at about four and a half billion years. This would fit right in with the idea that the universe developed over long ages of time in an evolutionary process.

But what the astronauts found, some believe, points to a much younger moon.

Tests conducted during the moon walks showed that the moon is still cooling. It has not yet solidified.

Other tests detected the presence of a magnetic field. This suggests that the moon has a fluid core, not a solid one—further support for the "young moon" idea.

The astronauts also registered moonquakes. Many thought the moon would be physically dead.

The most startling discovery was the small amount of cosmic moon dust the astronauts found. If the moon were four and one-half billion years old, then the cosmic dust, said some calculations, should have been fifty-four feet thick! Fearing the moon-landing module would sink into this deep powder, NASA spent billions of dollars trying to learn how thick the dust was.

But the layer of moon dust was shallow. Neil Armstrong, in fact, scuffed through to solid rock.

The Christian scientists called "scientific creationists" would say this moon evidence confirms their view that the world is only thousands of years old, not millions or billions. Whether or not you agree with that particular point of view, the moon facts can show you one thing. The evolutionary view of the universe that leaves out God is not a closed, proven case. The debate goes on. Someday you might even find some evidence to contribute!

Morse Code

The name of Samuel F. B. Morse made history the day in 1844 when he clicked a historic message from Washington, D.C. to Baltimore over a telegraph system that he had invented. In the "Morse Code" of dots and dashes (short and long clicks) that he had devised, Morse dispatched this brief message: "What hath God wrought!"

Samuel Morse found it easy to talk about God. His father, the Rev. Jedidiah Morse, was known as one of the strongest and most outspoken Christians of his day. And he was not just a preacher. He wrote the first geography book published in the United States and therefore became known as the "father of American geography."

Jedidiah Morse also was one of the first Americans to publish his religious views in tracts, and he spent his final years as a missionary to the Indians.

His son Samuel also had multiple talents. He earned fame as an accomplished artist before he was ever an inventor. His work *The Gallery of the Louvre* was sold in 1982 for $3.25 million—the most ever paid for an American painting.

Though other telegraph and code systems had been invented in Samuel Morse's time, his was the simplest and most efficient. But it took him twelve years to get it recognized! When it was finally put into wide use, Morse became a wealthy and famous man.

But he seemed to understand, as the words of his historic telegraph message imply, that God is behind all our talents and all our scientific discoveries.

Below is a listing of the dot and dash Morse codes used by telegraph operators for the letters of the alphabet. Probably the most famous telegraph signal is "SOS," short for, "Save our ship." Can you figure out how to signal it in code?

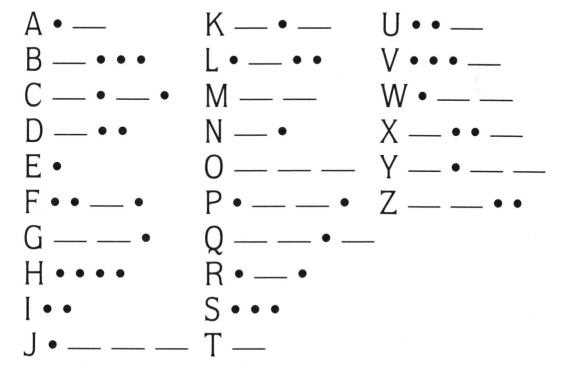

Most Popular Hymn

Can you name the most popular hymn in America?

A survey has revealed it to be "The Old Rugged Cross."

The composer, George Bennard, wrote the hymn in 1912 and then polished it up over the next year or two in the kitchen of his home in Albion, Michigan. He sang it along with his guitar.

Bennard appeared in the 1953 Rose Parade in Pasadena, California, aboard "The Old Rugged Cross" float. Near the front, on a flower-covered organ, he played his famous song for the largest live audience of his lifetime.

The next year, near his Reed City, Michigan home, the local Chamber of Commerce erected a twenty-foot-high, rough-hewn cross. In 1976, before his death, Bennard was named a member of the Gospel Music Hall of Fame.

Musicals for Kids

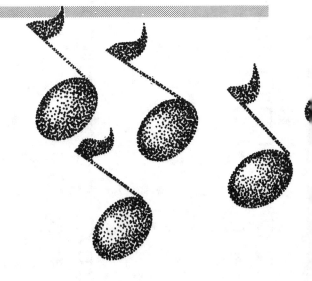

Christian recording companies have some great kids' albums on the market today. Some of them are full-fledged musicals designed for a whole group of kids—perhaps in your church—to learn and perform.

These musicals can be a lot of work, but they're also great fun. You can usually find them, on record or cassette, at your local Christian bookstore. Among the many on the market, here are just a few we especially recommend.

Bullfrogs & Butterflies (Birdwing). This illustrated Agapeforce album with story line narrated by Barry McGuire teaches children about relationships with parents, friends, and God. Songbook available.

Down by the Creek Bank (Impact). Dottie Rambo's album is a down-home, country-

Stevie and Nancy and the Music Machine (right) have sold so many of the Music Machine *album that it has earned a certified "Gold Record."*

style musical for children ages three to fourteen. Other available items include choral book, children's workbook, reel-to-reel accompaniment tape, bulletins, and an easy piano book for kids.

The Enchanted Journey (Light). This junior high level album is based on the story of John Bunyan's *Pilgrim's Progress.* Slides for multimedia presentations are also available.

It's Cool in the Furnace (Lexicon). The story of the three men God rescues from Nebuchadnezzar's fiery furnace comes alive here, with fun music in a variety of styles. Songbook available.

Kids Under Construction (Benson/Paragon). This musical from Bill and Gloria Gaither is designed to show kids of all ages the process of "becoming." It helps them understand growth and use God's Word as a blueprint for their lives.

Other items available include singer and director songbooks, reel-to-reel and cassette accompaniment tapes, conductor's score, orchestra parts, brass and rhythm parts, teacher's guide and resource manual, activity book, pin-on buttons, T-shirt transfers, and poster packet!

Kids Praise Album, 1, 2, and 3 (Maranatha Music). These albums contain praise songs for children. Other available items include songbooks and accompaniment on reel-to-reel or cassette tapes.

Klassics for Kids (Broadman). This album contains unison and two-part arrangements of music by great Christian composers. Especially for older children's choirs.

The Music Machine (Birdwing). One of the most popular musicals on the market. This Agapeforce album, complete with illustrations and story line, contains adventure and songs that teach the fruit of the Spirit. Songbook available.

Oh, the Joy of It (Broadman). This album contains unison and two-part arrangements of eight Buryl Red tunes especially for older children's choirs.

(See also *Christmas Sing-along.*)

Art courtesy of Agape Force

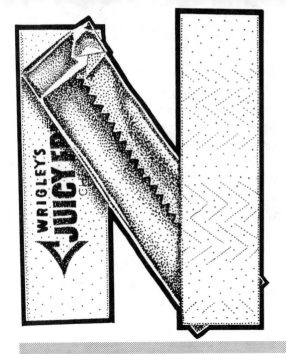

National Cathedral

The National Cathedral is one of three structures that dominate the Washington, D.C. skyline, along with the United States Capitol and the Washington Monument.

The massive Gothic cathedral looms on the highest point of land in the District of Columbia—Mount Saint Alban.

Though the church has been under construction for the past seventy-five years, it's not finished yet! Architects and builders keep expanding the huge complex, and adding new wings.

Every year a half million people come here from all over the world—to celebrate national days, to mourn a national or international leader, to tour the majestic structure, to worship in it.

Famous men are buried here—among them President Woodrow Wilson and the former admiral of the navy, George Dewey. It was also the site of funeral services for President Eisenhower. The Queen of England attended ceremonies here in 1976.

The cathedral's entryway is beautifully carved.

National Parks

The nice young fellow who pumps gas for you upon your arrival in a national park next summer may be the same one who preaches the sermon at the outdoor service there Sunday morning.

And the waitress who takes your order in the lodge restaurant may lead worshipers in a gospel hymn on the guitar.

Christian college students like these work for the park during the week. But at other times they may direct plays, lead choirs, organize recreation, teach Sunday school, or lead Bible studies.

You will find them in more than sixty national parks, forest, and resort areas across the nation. Their mission to vacationers has been going on now for more than thirty years, under the auspices of "A Christian Ministry in the National Parks."

One of the most unusual things these park workers do is their annual "Christmas in August" at Yellowstone, complete with public presentations of Handel's *Messiah*.

It may seem like a strange time of year to celebrate the birth of the Savior, but why not?

FREE! Parks Poster

Decorate your room with a 17-by-22-inch poster showing the exact location of the nearly forty national parks in the United States, plus a copy of *Our National Park System*, a leaflet which describes each of these parks. Write: Garden Club of America, 598 Madison Ave, New York, New York 10022. Enclose twenty-five cents for postage and handling.

Yellowstone National Park hosts Christmas in August.

Photo courtesy of the National Park Service

Nevada Steve

Does rodeo life sound exciting to you?

Meet "Nevada Steve" Homoki—ranch cook, stagecoach driver, and cowboy whip artist. He can tell you about excitement and danger—and also tell you that rodeo can't give you everything.

Born on a huge cattle ranch in Baker, Nevada, Steve Homoki learned early in life to ride a horse like a Comanche Indian. His riding landed him a job as a Hollywood stunt man with old-time western actors like Gary Cooper and Tom Mix. Later he toured the U.S. and Europe as a rope and whip artist, and followed the rodeo circuit.

In 1929, Nevada Steve rode the famous bucking horse, "Five Minutes to Midnight." He made the ride—one of the few who ever did! But before he could get off, the horse twisted in midair and came down backwards on him, breaking his back, neck, and twelve bones. Miraculously, he lived.

Later, Nevada Steve came to trust in Christ, and felt his life had been spared for a purpose. He went on to Chicago's Moody Bible Institute and for a while became a missionary among the Navajo Indians.

But for more than twenty years now, he has spent his summers entertaining teen-agers at the River Valley Ranch in Maryland (see *Ranches*). That's because there's nothing he'd rather do than help round up young people for Jesus.

Newspaper Delivery

Many famous people once began their careers as news carriers, or "paperboys." If you don't believe it, just visit the Freedoms Foundation at Valley Forge, and walk through their exhibit called "Famous Newspaper Carriers of America."

There you will find the photos and autographs of such famous Americans as World War II general Omar Bradley, former presidents Dwight Eisenhower and Jimmy Carter, and many others.

A good news carrier does more than deliver papers. Greg Enos (pictured at right)

was just twelve years old at the time he realized this and wrote the following—a news carrier's paraphrase of one of the Bible's most famous chapters, I Corinthians 13.

If I could do my paper route blindfolded,
> but did not have love for each one of my customers,
>> I would be just as well off
>> sitting in a closet the rest of my life.
> And if I could porch any house I wanted to,
>> using the backhand shot,
> and did not have love,
>> it would mean nothing.
> And if I could fold one hundred papers in five minutes,
>> but did not have love,
>> my time would be worthless.

Love is patient
> when you have to go back to a customer
>> five times to get him to pay you.
Love is kind
> when those mean kids in the court
>> throw their football at you
>>> when you're passing by.
Love isn't jealous
> when you hear of another paperboy making $150 a month
>> and you make only $50 a month.
Love is not proud
> when you have a history
>> of never throwing a paper on a roof
>> or breaking a window.
Love does not demand its own way
> when it's a rainy day
>> and you would rather have your parents drive you.

Tired, aching legs,
> rainy days,
> flat tires,
> and frightening dogs
>> will come to an end,
>>> but love is everlasting.
Customers that are difficult to please
> will come to an end,
>> but love is eternal.
Paper routes
> will come to an end,
>> but love never will.

Before I had my route,
> I thought only of my own desires.
But now I am aware of the need of a frail, old lady
> to be able to find her paper
>> on her porch on a dark night.
And of the weary businessman returning home
> to find his paper there on time.
These three things I have learned:
> endurance,
> patience,
> and love,
But the greatest of these is love.

Noah's Ark

In late summer of 1982, a nine-man expedition led by former *Apollo 15* astronaut Jim Irwin (see *Astronaut*), climbed Turkey's Mount Ararat in search of Noah's ark. The ark was not found. But on a national talk show after the climb, Irwin said there was no doubt in his mind that the ark is there.

The search for Noah's ark makes some people laugh or snicker. That's because they don't believe in the ark. They think it's just a "story" out of the Bible. They don't take the Book of Genesis as real history.

Yet for at least two centuries, reported sightings of the ark on Mount Ararat have persisted. Hundreds of reliable people, in fact, claim to have seen the ark. Here are just a few examples:

1853: Two Armenian natives showed the ark to three Englishmen.

1883: While examining the damage of a recent earthquake, Turkish investigators discovered the ark. The find was published in newspapers around the world.

1915, 1916: Two Russian flyers sighted the ark from the air. The czar dispatched 150 Russian soldiers and scientists to verify the claim. Ground investigators found the remains and succeeded in entering the three-storied structure and documenting it fully. However, when the Communists gained control, the documents disappeared, though many of the participants escaped the country and lived to tell the story.

1917: Six Turkish soldiers, returning home after service in Baghdad, decided to climb Mount Ararat. They accidentally discovered the ship.

1936: A New Zealand archaeologist accidentally discovered a field of timbers, very large and hand-hewn, on the upper slopes of the mountain.

1941-1944: At least three sightings were reported by World War II pilots: two Australian, one Russian, one American, and many more were rumored. The Air Force flyer took pictures of the ark, which appeared in the Tunisia edition of *Stars and Stripes*.

1948: A Kurdish farmer named Resit accidentally discovered the ark. At his insistence, many of his fellow villagers also observed it.

1952-1955: Fernand Navarra, wealthy French industrialist, found a great mass of hand-tooled lumber under the mountain's ice at thirteen thousand feet. He dug down to one nine-inch-thick beam, chopped off a portion about five feet long, and brought it back for analysis. The wood has been shown to be of great antiquity.

1953: George Greene, mining engineer for an American oil company, spotted the ark about one-third exposed from a helicopter. He photographed it from a distance

In Has Anybody Really Seen Noah's Ark?, Fernand Navarra poses with his "ark timber."

of about ninety feet. Although at least thirty people alive today remember the pictures, they can no longer be seen, for Greene was murdered in 1962 and his belongings were destroyed.

1969: Fernand Navarra returned to Mount Ararat and guided explorers to the spot of his discovery in 1955. Again fragments of wood were recovered.

By 1972, the search for Noah's ark began to intensify. But then, for a variety of reasons, Turkey closed off access to most search parties. Mount Ararat is on the Russian border, and has long been a sensitive defense area.

Speculation about this mysterious object took another surge in 1977 when Sun Classic Pictures, producers of *The Life and Times of Grizzly Adams*, released the film *In Search of Noah's Ark*.

The movie contends that the ark origi-nally rested at the sixteen-thousand-foot level, but that in 1940 it broke in half because of a strong earthquake. Part of it slid down the mountain to the fourteen-thousand-foot level, leaving sections of wood thrown about the area. This may have been where Navarra retrieved his wood samples in 1955 and 1969.

With all of this promising circumstantial evidence, why is it not possible simply to climb the mountain and prove the ark's existence once and for all?

It's not as easy as it would seem.

Though not the world's highest mountain, the seventeen-thousand-foot Ararat is one of the world's largest in sheer size.

The mountain is a dangerous one to climb. Flowing glaciers erode volcanic lava underneath. The slopes are steep. Shifting boulders abound, and sometimes even the sound of a voice or a step in the wrong

Photo courtesy of Creation Life Publications

place can start an avalanche.

The object believed to be the ark is under ice and snow most of the year, which leaves only a short period of time each year for serious search.

The Kurdish tribes who live on the mountain are often unfriendly to outsiders. Grizzly bears, mountain lions, and wolves live in rock fissures and caves up to the ice line. Lower regions are infested by snakes.

The weather at higher elevations can be fierce. Sudden storms erupt, even on what may start out to be a nice day. On one such occasion, an expedition of three men took shelter on a large rock. Lightning struck, and two of the men were hurtled off the rock. One was frozen in place by electrical force. Though momentarily paralyzed by the high voltage, they all recovered.

Former astronaut Jim Irwin didn't have it easy either. He tripped and tumbled down the mountainside, and had to be evacuated to a hospital by helicopter.

Stolen equipment, denied permits, sickness, and other frustrations have seemingly plagued many of the expeditions in search of Noah's ark. "Why such resistance?" one might ask. Is it from God or Satan?

Most Christians are convinced that if the ark is found at all, it will not be until God's own timing. Certainly our trust in the accuracy of the Bible from beginning to end should not depend upon its discovery.

But Dr. Melville Grosvenor, the late editor of *National Geographic,* said that the ark would be "the greatest archaeological find of history."

It would be even more than that, say scientists of the Institute for Creation Research. The ark would be evidence of a catastrophic worldwide flood that restructured the crust of the earth in fairly recent times. This would challenge the evolutionist premise that the earth's surface was shaped gradually over millions of years.

Discovery of the ark would also certainly document dramatically the accuracy of the Bible, even in its oldest historic details.

There is other evidence, of course, that already points to the idea of a worldwide flood. The earth's land surface is more than 75 percent sedimentary. Ocean fossils have been found on top of some of the world's highest mountains—among them Mt. Everest, the Rockies, and the Andes!

Legends and stories of a devastating flood can be found all over the world—from the Eskimos to the Australian aborigines, from the Chinese to the South American Indians. While the details vary, all

Ararat's Upper Gorge is a treacherous spot.

of them at least somewhat resemble the story of Noah and his escape from the waters in a ship.

Other questions about the ark, of course, persist.

"How could Noah accomplish such an engineering feat in his time?" The civilization was probably much more advanced than most think.

"How did Noah round up all the animals?" The Bible says he didn't have to. God caused the animals to come to *him*.

"How could the ark have held all the animals?" Scientists calculate from the measurements the Bible records that it could have held the cargo of 569 railroad freight cars.

"In such a catastrophe, wouldn't the boat have capsized?" A study of its structure has revealed that collapse would have been almost impossible.

Yet most skeptics will never be satisfied. The author of *The Christian Kids Almanac* heard such a point of view recently. In half jest, the man asked how in the world anyone could identify the ark anyway. "I'm sure Noah didn't put his name on it," he asserted. "And the animal droppings would be long gone by now." It was obvious he considered it all a myth, and had dismissed it as simply that.

But if a large boat were found at that elevation on Mount Ararat, I thought, *what else might it be?* Surely not the *Nina,* the *Pinta,* or the *Santa Maria!*

And if some prankster had simply tried to plant such an object on the peak, it would have been one tremendous job!

Besides, the exact measurements of the ark are in the Bible. The cubits it records translate into a vessel 450 feet long, 75 feet wide, and 45 feet tall. The Scriptures even describe a skylight around the top, eighteen inches below the roof.

If the ark were found even partially intact, it should be possible to get some measurements or architectural evidence that would verify the find.

Would not the ark have deteriorated by now? Ordinarily, yes. But consider how an entombment in ice and snow at that altitude might have preserved the ark for our discovery thousands of years later!

Is it really the ark? Only time will tell.

Meanwhile Jim Irwin intends to keep looking for it. But while recovering from his injuries from his fall down Ararat, he told reporters that next time he may do his searching from a plane!

Photo courtesy of Creation Life Publications

Nobel Prize Nominee

In 1982 Dr. Kenneth Pike, Wycliffe Bible Translators' foremost linguist, was nominated for the famous Nobel Peace Prize.

Wycliffe missionaries serve around the world, translating the Bible into native languages.

And Dr. Pike is looked upon by Wycliffe and by others around the world as one of the greatest linguistic geniuses of all.

Pike has developed a system with which, in only one hour's time, he can crack the secrets of an unknown language—just as one might crack a mysterious code.

A typical demonstration of the method before an audience of linguists goes something like this:

Dr. Pike stands onstage, surrounded by blackboards. On a small table close by are

Photo courtesy of Wycliffe Bible Translators

A young Ken takes local transportation in Mexico.

several sticks, leaves, and similar objects.

A woman walks onstage. Pike greets her in Mixtec, a language of Mexico she has never heard before. She responds in another language that Pike has never heard before. He carefully repeats her words, then whirls around to the blackboard.

He scribbles down the words in a phonetic alphabet. They mean "hello."

Using gestures, Pike invites her to sit

down, and the real fun begins. With Mixtec as his launching pad, he waves a leaf and gestures until the woman understands that he wants to know how to say, "It's a leaf," in her language. He scribbles the expression down and goes on to "one leaf," "two leaves," "my leaf," "your leaf." He sits down, stands up, leaps around, all the time eliciting words from his new friend.

Soon he can put together nouns and verbs to form sentences. Before the hour is over, he has analyzed a good share of the grammar and started a dictionary. He's sorted out the sounds of the language and created a tentative alphabet. And he's done all this without resorting to English or any other language which he and the woman volunteer both understand.

It's a good show. But the real purpose of Pike's system is to help missionaries translate the Bible into unknown languages.

The brilliant scholar often reminds fellow Christians that God commands us to love him not only with all our hearts but also with all our minds (Mark 12:30).

It was because of his great contribution to linguistics that he was nominated for the Nobel Peace Prize. The honor is sure to advance the cause of Bible translators around the globe.

Interestingly, the Nobel Peace Prize was founded by the Swedish chemist who invented dynamite. Alfred Nobel felt so guilty about inventing something that could be used for violence that he left part of his fortune to be awarded to those working for peace.

For more on the Wycliffe translators, see the interesting story of *Uncle Cam*.

Noisemakers

Mom tells you not to slam the door. Dad complains about the loud tv or radio. Sound familiar? Parents, it seems, are always worrying about noise.

They are not the only ones, though. So is the United States government. They're out to do something about the noise level, especially in American cities.

Jackhammers and cars are big noise offenders. Memphis, Tennessee, has long had an ordinance against "unreasonable noise." Hundreds of honking motorists have been fined. Now almost no one in that city blows a horn anymore.

The government wants manufacturers to make their products quieter, and many already have. But buyers sometimes seem to think that if a vacuum cleaner, or sports car, or motorcycle isn't noisy enough, it isn't any good. They'll even buy the typewriter tha makes more of a *clack*.

A power lawn mower generates about 96 decibels, an amplified rock band 115, and a jet plane at takeoff 150. For the average person, a noise of 130 decibels causes pain. A continuous noise level above 85 decibels, science has found, can and does cause hearing loss.

When there's too much noise, often others can't get through to us. Nor can God when other goings-on in our lives drown him out.

Perhaps that's why the Bible says, "Be still, and know that I am God" (Psalm 46:10).

OceanTravelers

The ships you see in the photos on this page are among the most unusual ships in the world. Why? Their crews are made of Christian young people from more than thirty nations, and they sail the world with the gospel of Jesus. Over a million people visit the ships each year.

The *Logos* (Greek for *word*), nearly a football field in length, carries a crew and staff of 140 young people. Since it was purchased in 1970 by a Christian group called Operation Mobilization, it has spent time in the ports of seventy countries. While in port, the crew members talk about Christ in the city and countryside, hand out literature, work with schools and churches, and sell Christian books. In 1982 the *Logos* sailed primarily among the countries of the Middle East.

The *Doulos* (Greek for *servant*) is almost twice the size of the *Logos*. Built in 1914 and acquired by Operation Mobilization for a bargain $770,000, the ship got a new engine in 1970. It has a crew of three hundred, including forty children. One of its huge decks has been turned into a large exhibition hall of books, and when it is in port people come aboard to buy. It also has many classrooms, and hosts about 180,000 people in conferences each year. In 1982 it sailed primarily among the ports of Latin America.

These ships have made an impact all around the world. Em, a Filipino with Operation Mobilization, says he was far from the sea once, crossing the Sahara Desert, and met a young boy who asked, "Do you know anything about the ship *Logos*?" When Em nodded, the boy said, "I thought so. Four years ago you gave a program in my school in Ethiopia. Please keep giving that program."

It takes a lot of work and skill to sail a ship. The captain of the *Doulos* is a man with many years of experience on the sea, who once captained an even larger ship. Ninety others on board are professional seamen.

Still another ship floating the waters for Jesus is the 11,695-ton *Anastasis* (Greek for *resurrection*). It was purchased in 1978 and then refurbished by Youth with a Mission (YWAM), which each year sends some ten thousand young people into locations all around the world for short-term missions. (See *Youth with a Mission.*)

The *Anastasis* has five cargo holds for

Anastasis

Logos

Life on the Doulos *involves work in the galley.*

relief materials and food, an eighteen-bed hospital, classrooms, and auditoriums. It docked at Guatemala in January 1983 to aid Operation Love Lift, a cooperative Christian outreach to that nation. It then sailed to New Zealand and the Pacific islands. Its prime arena for service will be in Asia and the Pacific.

It may seem extravagant for Christians to buy and maintain their own fleet of ships. But because these ships provide lodging, relief cargo space, classroom space, and transportation, and have high mobility, they have been calculated to be some of the least expensive missionary outreaches on a per person basis. The ships have access to much of the world's population: seven of the ten most populous cities of the world are port cities. So it makes sense after all.

And that's why thousands of Christians today, many of them youth, are sailing the high seas for Jesus.

Oregon Trailblazers

On the banks of the Mississippi River at St. Louis, the huge Gateway Arch soars into the sky, framing the city's skyline from miles away.

St. Louis used to be the spot "where the West began," and this monument celebrates the trek of over 300,000 men, women, and children in history's largest overland migration: the Oregon Trail.

The historic trail began here, where pioneers loaded their covered wagons, chose a trail boss, and headed out across two thousand miles of mud and dust, mountain and plain.

Some of the earliest to blaze the Oregon Trail were missionaries.

Stirred by accounts of explorers and traders, missionaries had become interested in the Oregon country—which at that time included what is now Washington state—as early as the 1820s. But the remoteness of the area discouraged them.

Then in 1833, a magazine article described the visit to St. Louis of some western Indians seeking teachers and the white man's "Book of Heaven"—the Bible. In New York State, Marcus Whitman, a doctor, and his young bride, Narcissa, were among the first to respond to their plea.

In 1835, Marcus Whitman journeyed to the Rockies with the American Fur Company caravan, and concluded, "Where wagons could go, women could go." Actually a wagon had never yet rumbled all the way to Oregon. But the doctor was determined to try, both with the wagon and his wife, in spite of the warnings of friends.

The journey took seven months, and proved extremely difficult. The Whitmans

had to contend with sick companions, a slow-moving cattle herd, and an unwieldly wagon. Marcus had to leave his wagon—reduced to a two-wheeled cart—at Fort Boise before crossing the Blue Mountains, where he could follow only the trails of Indians and trappers.

Through all of this Narcissa continued to trust in the Lord. We know the depth of her faith because she kept a diary on the trek, which was later recovered for future generations to read. Along with another missionary wife, Eliza Spalding, she became the first white woman to cross the Rockies. Rockies.

The Whitmans finally arrived safely and opened a mission among the Cayuse at their landmark outpost. They learned the Indian language, devised an alphabet, and at the same time graciously hosted travelers on the Oregon Trail. Narcissa taught school and handled endless nursing chores.

But after a few years, as the flow of white settlers into the Northwest increased, troubles erupted.

On November 29, 1847, a band of Cayuse attacked the mission and killed Marcus Whitman, his wife, and nearly a dozen others. A few survivors escaped, and fifty at the mission station were taken captive.

News of the tragedy sped to Congress in Washington, D.C., along with petitions from the settlers that the U.S. promptly establish territorial rule in the tense Northwest wilderness. Congress acted, and the Oregon Territory emerged.

Though the Whitmans gave their lives for the cause of the gospel, their testimony lived on. The site of their missionary outpost, near present-day Walla Walla, Washington, is now a national historic landmark.

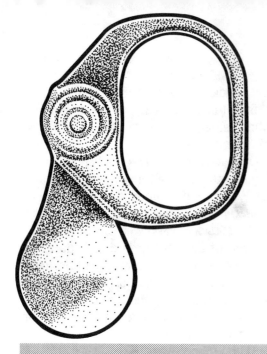

Peanut Wizard

When someone says "peanuts," whose name do you think of first?

You would probably say Jimmy Carter.

But there was another famous man much more important to peanuts: George Washington Carver.

Henry Ford once called Carver "the world's greatest living scientist."

Carver not only taught the South how to grow peanuts, but also what to do with them. He discovered more than three hundred products that could be made from peanuts—everything from "coffee" to sand and feathers!

Carver was born a slave in 1864, then orphaned as a child. He had poor health. Everything seemed against him. But at an early age he came to know Jesus as his Savior, and he always took his spiritual life seriously.

He was the first black man to study at Iowa State, where he earned highest honors and a master's degree. But he turned down an offer to teach there in order to serve his people at Tuskegee Institute in Alabama. There he devised not only hundreds of uses for peanuts, but also for

Photo courtesy of Tuskegee Institute

sweet potatoes and soybeans.

Carver's ability in agricultural chemistry led to much of his fame and popularity, but he had other talents as well. He was also an artist and musician.

Once members of Congress asked Carver how he managed to accomplish so much. After a moment's pause, he answered, "At four o'clock each morning I sit down and ask the Creator what I am to do that day. Then I go ahead and do it."

Pearl Harbor

On Sunday morning, December 7, 1941, a major part of the United States Pacific fleet rested lazily at anchor in Pearl Harbor, Hawaii. Meanwhile, a squadron of nearly two hundred Japanese war planes streaked in from the north, ready to deliver its devastating blow.

Commanding the squadron was Captain Mitsuo Fuchida, wearing around his flying cap a white headband with a red circle—the Japanese rising sun. Fuchida kept his planes low—a mere three thousand meters above the water—to duck the enemy's radar.

Upon sighting the American fleet, he called for the attack: "Tora! Tora! Tora!"

An hour later, more than two thousand Americans were dead, the United States fleet had been largely destroyed, and the nation remained only hours away from official entry into World War II.

Fuchida's mission had succeeded. But that isn't all. There is a remarkable twist to the story of this Japanese captain.

When word of the sneak attack Fuchida had led flashed over the radio that morning at an army camp mess hall in California, Sergeant Jake DeShazer flew into a rage and hurled a potato against the wall. "Just wait and see what we'll do to you!" he shouted at the enemy.

DeShazer later flew in a secret raid on Tokyo, but he had to parachute into hostile territory near Nanking and wound up a prisoner of war. DeShazer's hatred boiled for more than two years, until one cold winter day when someone passed a Bible through his cell group. DeShazer began to study it, his heart began to soften, and in time he asked the Lord into his life.

Meanwhile, Fuchida, who had hoped to become an admiral, saw his dreams fade as he sat out the Battle of Midway with appendicitis and learned that ten Japanese warships had gone down.

At the end of the war, DeShazer earned his degree at Seattle Pacific University, a Christian school, and returned to Japan as a missionary.

Fuchida found himself out of work. Worried about the war trials to be held for the

Japanese military, he returned to farming near Osaka. But though General MacArthur summoned him to the trials, it was not as a defendant, but only as a witness.

One day in 1950, as Fuchida got off a train in a Tokyo station, an American handed him a pamphlet. Its title: "I Was a Prisoner of Japan." Fuchida stuck it in his pocket and read it later. It was Sergeant Jake DeShazer's dramatic story.

Fuchida could not explain, nor forget, what he had read. Though a Buddhist by tradition, he bought a Bible and began to search it.

The drama of the crucifixion impressed him, especially Christ's prayer shortly before his death: "Father, forgive them, for they know not what they do." The message hit him hard. He had slaughtered so many!

On April 12, 1950, Fuchida became a Christian. The news shocked his family and made newspaper headlines. Old war buddies tried to destroy his new faith. Many said it wouldn't last.

But Fuchida continued to speak out for Jesus and conducted crusades throughout Japan. For more than a quarter century, until shortly before his death in 1978, he continued to preach the gospel in his home country, in the United States, and on other continents, often in the presence of world leaders.

DeShazer appeared with Fuchida many times. The two soldiers, who had so many reasons to hate one another, would join together to demonstrate the power of the Prince of Peace!

Penney, J.C.

The late J. C. Penney, son of a Baptist minister, learned honesty from his father. He adopted the Golden Rule as his business ethic, and in a few years built his store chain into one of the nation's giants— worth forty million dollars.

Then in 1929, the stock market crashed. Penney's fortune crashed with it. By 1932 Penney had to sell out to pay his debts. It left him almost bankrupt. The trauma affected his health, and he wound up in a hospital in Battle Creek, Michigan.

Early one morning, Penney woke to hear the distant singing of employees who had gathered to start the day praising God.

They were singing these words: "Be not dismayed, whate'er betide; God will take care of you ..."

Penney followed the music down the hallway to its source, a chapel, and slipped into the back row.

When he left a short time later he was a changed man, and ready to start the long climb back to health.

Penney then rebuilt his chain of department stores across America into a much greater empire than it had ever been before. He gave much of his new fortune to Christian causes.

Pennsylvania

Your school may have taught you the name of William Penn, the man who founded Pennsylvania ("Penn's woods"). You probably learned that he was a Quaker, and that he promoted Pennsylvania to peoples far and wide as a land of liberty.

But what was his motive?

William Penn received the land as an inheritance. His father had been Admiral Sir William Penn, who, among other exploits, had discovered the island of Bermuda. The English government owed the elder Penn a large sum of money, which in turn was to be passed on to his son.

But young William had another idea. Instead of a cash settlement, he petitioned the king for a tract of land in America "lying north of Maryland, on the east bounded with Delaware River, on the west limited as Maryland is, and northward to extend as far as plantable, which is altogether Indian."

The venture might at first sound like a greedy son out to gamble his father's wealth on a wild speculative land scheme. But note the young man's driving motive as he writes to a friend:

"I do, therefore, desire the Lord's wisdom to guide me, and those that may be concerned with me, that we do the thing that is truly wise and just."

The king gave to Penn what later became one of the largest states in the northeast United States, with the right to govern. A year later the Duke of York also gave Penn what is now Delaware.

Penn clearly saw all of this as a trust from God. "I eyed the Lord in obtaining it," he wrote, "and more was I drawn inward to look to him, and to owe it to his hand and power than to any other way. I have so obtained it, and desire to keep it that I may not be unworthy of his love."

A man of lesser character might have squandered this huge piece of real estate to the detriment of generations to come. But not Penn. He perceived that the God who had "given it me through many difficulties, will, I believe, bless and make it the seed of a nation." As a Quaker who had experienced persecution, he saw the colony as a haven for the persecuted, a land of religious freedom. So he wrote advertisements for his colony, printed them in six languages, and sent them to Europe.

Into Pennsylvania poured the Dutch, the Swedes, the Welsh, English Quakers, German groups, and, last of all, the Scotch-Irish—all people under religious or economic oppression.

Pennsylvania did, in fact, become "the seed of a nation."

FREE: Pennsylvania Map

Learn more about the state founded by William Penn. Send for a colorful brochure and free road map of Pennsylvania. Write: Department of Commerce, Bureau of Travel Development, Room 206, South Office Building, Harrisburg, Pennsylvania 17120.

Photography: Kids at Work

With the sophisticated, simple-to-operate cameras made these days, photography is a hobby any kid can take up with nice results. As with any skill, the more you practice and study, the better you become. And what's nice about the skill of photography is that it can develop into a Christian ministry—and even a career.

Take seventeen-year-old David Flood of Olympia Fields, Illinois, for example. He started snapping pictures in the sixth grade with an inexpensive camera, then borrowed his dad's 35mm camera (with permission, of course). By ninth grade he had sold eight photos to Christian book publishers, one to a Christian magazine, and two to his local newspaper. (The photos went with articles others had written.)

David's youth pastor encouraged him to create multimedia shows (slides and music) for the church. Two missionaries home on furlough asked him to take new family photos for their prayer cards. He's now sold enough photos to buy his own 35mm camera and several hundred dollars of equipment to go with it! David doesn't know yet, but what started out as a hobby may turn into a career.

Some Christian publishers and mission groups employ photographers full-time, and have them travel to get pictures for their books and magazines. Many other Christian groups use free-lance photographers.

Interested in trying photography yourself?

Two major Christian youth magazines conduct annual photo contests, and you can learn a lot by entering, and by studying the work of the winners. *Young Ambassador* magazine's contest is open only to kids high school age or younger; *Campus Life* magazine's may include older competitors. For information, write to:

- Contest, *Young Ambassador*, Box 82808, Lincoln, Nebraska 68501.
- *Campus Life* Photo Contest, 465 Gundersen Drive, Carol Stream, Illinois 60187.

Matt Cooper's rugby photo won a prize from Campus Life.

Photography: 3-D Camera

They said it couldn't be done—that it was impossible, or at least impractical. Yet now the world of photography has been revolutionized by the 3-D camera—one so simple even an amateur can handle it.

This camera has added a whole new dimension to the photographic scene. The color prints you get back have depth—as if you should be able to reach your hand back into the picture.

The man behind the Nimslo 3-D camera is Jerry Nims, who only six years ago appeared to be on the verge of bankruptcy. Though blazing a trail in photo technology, he could barely pay his staff of nine researchers. So as a Christian, he prayed hard.

In 1978 came the break. He was able to raise more than $100 million to produce and market the Nimslo (named for Nims and Allen Lo, the Chinese technician behind the invention). Today Nims is the chairman and chief executive officer of the Nimslo Corporation. In 1982 his company was valued at $450 million!

Nims calls his sudden success "a flat-out miracle."

There's more to the story. Nims gives much of his profits from the camera to Christian causes. This includes Christian book projects and Christian programs to help the poor in the cities of Atlanta and Denver. He also is helping the persecuted Christians of Eastern Europe.

Nims knows his money is only a trust from God, and that he has an obligation to help those less fortunate. So he keeps four pictures of refugees on his office wall. He looks at them each day, he says, to remind himself that other people go to bed hungry.

Picture Bible

Most kids like comic books, or turn to the comics in the newspaper. Despite the word "comics," not all of them are comedy. But all are easy to read.

That's why, many years ago, the publishers of *The Christian Kids Almanac* decided to put Bible stories into picture-strip form. Readers could then see the action, and Bible events would come to life.

The stories first appeared in *Sunday Pix*, a Sunday school take-home paper that became the largest Christian children's weekly, with a North American circulation of one million. Later the stories were bound into a volume called *The Picture Bible*.

The artist who did *The Picture Bible*, Andre LeBlanc, worked hard to draw everything accurately: the landscape, the clothing and armor worn

in biblical times, the height and width of city walls, and many other details. He did extensive research, and even traveled to Israel.

He also had to decide how to portray the major characters of the Bible—like the rough outdoorsman Peter, and the brilliant scholar Paul, and many more.

The Picture Bible has since been put into 150 different languages, and is now read by young and old all over the world.

GOLIATH'S DEAD!

Piltdown Man

Thirty years ago, almost every school-child in America believed in the Piltdown man.

This was the name given to some bones found around 1910 in a gravel pit near Piltdown Common, England. Scientists were sure at the time that they had found an

ancestor to man: a curious fossil with a humanlike cranium and an apelike jaw that was a link in the evolutionary chain.

Instead, it turned out to be one of the greatest hoaxes of history.

In 1953, after more than forty years, new analytic techniques revealed the skull to be a fraud. It had been artificially aged by potassium bichromate!

But who did it? And why?

In 1979, *Time* magazine reported that scientists may have identified the culprit: the late William Johnson Sollas, an Oxford University professor who was a pillar of British science in the early 1900s.

But what could have been his motive?

Sollas, reported *Time*, may have wanted to destroy the reputation of a hated rival scientist—Arthur Smith Woodward. So he decided to trick him into publicly accepting as authentic what would later be unmasked as an elaborate joke.

The evidence suggests that Sollas ordered a packet of potassium bichromate by mail and borrowed ape teeth from the Oxford anatomy department's collection.

Having "doctored" the skull, it seems, he "planted" it in a gravel pit where archaeological excavations were already underway. Sooner or later, he knew, it would be found.

The hoax worked beautifully. But it eventually backfired on Sollas.

"The Piltdown man," says *Time*, "was accepted not only by Smith Woodward, but by almost the entire scientific establishment." With such eminent names authenticating the find, Sollas chose to remain silent, for it would have been "unseemly for a man in his position to admit such a trick."

Meanwhile, because of this professor's prank and the gullibility of his fellow scientists, millions of schoolchildren were taught that the Piltdown man was scientific evidence for human evolution.

It was quickly pulled from school textbooks around the world after the embarrassing discovery in 1953. Piltdown was not the first ancient "man," however, who has turned out to be something else.

The bone fragments once thought to be "Nebraska man" turned out to be a pig's tooth!

Scientists once declared the stooped "Neanderthal man" to be a link between man and ape. Later analysis revealed the man simply had a disease called rickets!

Pioneer Clubs

Pioneer Clubs is a Christian organization for boys and girls grades one through twelve, found in many churches across America. In the United States there are five thousand clubs with a total of sixty thousand club members. Canada also has the program.

he clubs (Pioneer Boys and Pioneer Girls) usually meet after school or in the evening. Kids play games, learn skills and crafts, sing songs, read the Bible and have lots of fun.

The Pioneer Clubs also have twenty-six camps across America, each one called Camp Cherith. It publishes a magazine

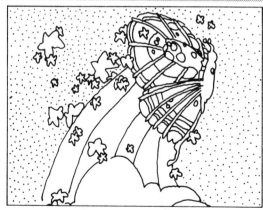

called *Trails* for elementary aged readers.

For more information about Pioneer Clubs and the ones nearest you, write: Pioneer Ministries, Box 788, Wheaton, Illinois 60187.

Play by Play

Roman soldiers, mounted on proud Arabian horses, arrogantly ride through the teeming city street, forcing the populace into the path of a passing camel caravan. Pigeons escape from cages as merchants and moneylenders are driven from the Temple.

The action is not in Jerusalem, but at Spearfish, South Dakota, a small western town not far from the gold rush city of Deadwood or the famous Mount Rushmore.

Each summer on this site more than two hundred actors and actresses in authentic costumes dramatize the life of Jesus three times a week. The famed Black Hills Passion Play has been drawing crowds since 1939.

The original cast was from Germany, but they had such difficulty speaking the English language that many eventually gave up and returned to Europe.

But not Josef Meier, who plays the role of Jesus. You can still see him perform each summer in the Black Hills Passion Play. Today he is proclaimed by critics in the United States and abroad as the outstanding interpreter of this most difficult role. So far, he has given more than six thousand performances!

FREE: Drama Resources Catalog

Many church youth groups enjoy performing Christian dramas. But where do you find good plays, skits, monologues, and the like? Simply write for the *Catalog of Hard-to-Find Christian Participation Resources,* published by Contempory Drama Service, Box 457-WZ, Downers Grove, Illinois 60515. Its forty-eight pages describe hundreds of skits and where to get them—plus resources for puppets, clowns, and mime. You'll also learn how to get free sampler kits of Christian sketches from the Jeremiah People, a traveling Christian drama troupe.

Poetry

It takes special ability—and a love of words—to write good poetry. Often this ability shows up at an early age. Luci Shaw, author of three volumes of poetry on life from the Christian's point of view, did a lot of reading and writing when she was young. She began winning poetry contests as a teen. Luci feels her poems are gifts she offers to God. Here's a sample from one of her books, *Listen to the Green.* It's called "Reluctant Prophet."

> Both were dwellers
> in deep places (one
> in the dark bowels
> of ships and great fish
> and wounded pride.
> The other
> in the silvery belly
> of the seas). Both
> heard God saying
> "Go!"
> but the whale
> did as he was told.

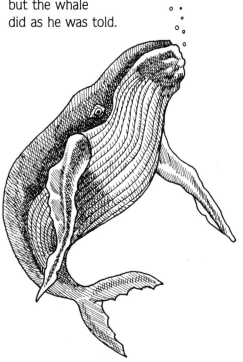

If you like to write poetry, and would like to try to get some of it in print, you have several possible outlets. *Young Ambassador* magazine has an annual poetry contest. *Trails* magazine, a publication of Pioneer Ministries, will consider your poetry for publication, as will the Sunday school papers *Sprint* and *Teen Power.* (Addresses are listed below.) Your local church paper or your denomination's publications may also consider your work.

Here's one sample of a young person's poem in print. Thirteen-year-old Matt Elliott of Wheaton, Illinois had this poem published in a March 1983 issue of *Sprint.* It's called "Peter's Song," about Jesus' disciple by that name.

> Peace
> The beautiful peace of the sea
> All alone on my sailboat
> The rocking of the deep blue sea
> Subdues me.
> Crying gulls
> And flying fish
> Or better yet
> The smell of frying fish
> Perfectly soothes
> My restless spirit.

If you'd like to read more of Luci Shaw's poetry, ask at your Christian bookstore for one of her three books: *Listen to the Green, The Secret Trees,* or *The Sighting,* all from Harold Shaw Publishers.

If you want to attempt to get your own poetry published, try these periodicals:

Sprint, David C. Cook Publishing, 850 N. Grove Avenue, Elgin, Illinois 60120.

Teen Power, Scripture Press, Box 513, Glen Ellyn, Illinois 60137.

Trails, Box 788, Wheaton, Illinois 60187.

Young Ambassador, Box 82808, Lincoln, Nebraska 68501.

Price, Michelle

Michelle Price was only eight years old when her left leg had to be amputated at the knee because of bone cancer.

She might have felt sorry for herself and given up on life and on God. But she didn't. Michelle had a strong faith in Jesus Christ. She was determined to make the best of a tough situation.

And that is exactly what she has done.

She has learned to ski, roller-skate, and ride a horse!

In the 1980 Handicap National Ski Championships, she won a gold medal in slalom.

Michelle doesn't want people to feel funny about her because of her leg. Within only a few days after her surgery, she drew funny little faces on the bandages covering the stump. And when asked about what happened to her limb, she would come back with quips like, "My leg? Oh, I was in a swamp and an alligator got it."

Despite her own problems, she seems much more concerned about others than herself. She has not lost her zest for life.

In 1978, Michelle won a "Victor's Award" from the City of Hope, where she

Photo courtesy of Regal Books

had been hospitalized. It was presented to her by Wayne Newton, who also gave her a regal Arabian horse, "Prince," from his own prize collection of beautiful horses!

If you'd like to read more about this courageous girl, her story is told in the book, *Michelle*, by Carolyn Phillips (Regal Books).

Property Switches

At some time or other, you and your friends have probably turned something like an old doghouse or toolshed into a playhouse. It's fun to change a building from one use to another.

Churches and other Christian groups have ended up with some interesting property as a result of such switches.

● Famed evangelist Dwight L. Moody once turned a beer hall into a Sunday school.

● One large church met for some years in a movie theater auditorium.

● Some congregations have turned old barns into churches. One such church in McHenry, Illinois, made the silo into the pastor's office!

The international headquarters of Campus Crusade for Christ at Arrowhead Springs, California, was once a plush resort hotel for the Hollywood celebrity circuit. In later years, when the celebrities migrated to other places like Palm Springs, it fell into disuse. Campus Crusade acquired it for a remarkable price and turned it into a Christian training center.

Another resort hotel—on Lookout Mountain in Tennessee—was, at some points in its history, the site of gambling and underworld activity. Some women in the nearby town prayed that the hotel would house a Christian school. When the resort later fell into financial trouble, it was purchased by Covenant College.

The Navigators, a well-known Christian organization headquartered near Colorado Springs, has as its main base of operation a sixty-seven room, sandstone, Tudor-style *castle*. A tunnel, secret panels, and a massive tower overlooking a moat add old-world atmosphere.

The castle was built by William Jackson Palmer, the Civil War's youngest general,

The Navigators' "castle" is known as Glen Eyrie.

who moved west to found Colorado Springs and build the Denver and Rio Grande Railroad. The Navigators bought the building in 1953 at a bargain price.

Puppets

Everyone's heard of the haughty Miss Piggy, the hungry Cookie Monster, and the patient frog Kermit. The Muppets have proven that puppets are popular with all ages.

The Claypool family of Vista, California, are convinced that puppetry is also a great way to share the gospel. The entire family of eight—five daughters, one son—gets in on the act, and they've taken their "C. C. Puppet Tree" routines into schools, churches, even a military base.

Mom Claypool, who took a course in puppets at a nearby college, makes most of the puppets, writes the scripts, and works a few hand puppets. Dad is the sound and stage man, and sometimes crawls inside "Ted," a "walking" puppet. Daughter Cherrie emcees. Colleen is "Perky," a firefly who wants to learn more about the Bible. And so it goes, with Cathy, Correen, Cindy, and Cliff each playing their special parts with puppets like Jim Turkey, Funny Bones,

The whole Claypool family gets in on the puppet act.

Goliath, Ug, and Malo.

Their programs run from thirty to forty-five minutes, and include humor as well as Bible truth. Even after the Claypools learn a routine, they usually rehearse for about four hours before a show.

If you want to take up puppetry as a hobby, you can find a nice selection of puppets in many of today's Christian bookstores. They usually also stock books on the how-to of puppetry: puppet making, staging, and scriptwriting. For a free catalog about other drama resources, see *Play by Play*.

Puzzles

Most kids like puzzles, but some are even good at making them. Matt Kauffman of Indiana, age twelve, created this rather elaborate crossword puzzle on the books of the Old Testament. It was published in the *Young Ambassador* magazine. You will find the answers on page 224.

The word find of Old Testament books was created by Dean Wenger, age fourteen, of Pennsylvania. The answers are on page 224.

If you'd like to try your hand at puzzle making, you can enter *Young Ambassador's* annual contest. Write for information to: Contest, *Young Ambassador*, Box 82808, Lincoln, Nebraska 68501.

The Books of the Old Testament:

Genesis	Exodus
Leviticus	Numbers
Deuteronomy	Joshua
Judges	Ruth
I and II Samuel	I and II Kings
I and II Chronicles	Ezra
Nehemiah	Esther
Job	Psalms
Proverbs	Ecclesiastes
Song of Solomon	Isaiah
Jeremiah	Lamentations
Ezekiel	Daniel
Hosea	Joel
Amos	Obadiah
Jonah	Micah
Nahum	Habakkuk
Zephaniah	Haggai
Zechariah	Malachi

Find all the books of the Old Testament in the Word Find—either horizontally, vertically, backwards or diagonally. Then, to find a hidden message, write the uncircled letters as you see them from left to right, starting at the top.

```
H  A  B  A  K  K  U  K  B  S  M  L  A  S  P  O
H  A  U  O  L  K  M  I  C  A  H  A  S  U  J  N
R  A  I  H  L  E  O  J  L  M  A  M  S  C  U  A
U  E  I  M  S  O  I  A  F  U  I  E  R  I  D  H
T  X  E  D  E  O  C  K  T  E  M  N  E  T  G  U
H  O  S  E  A  H  J  H  E  L  E  T  B  I  E  M
A  D  T  E  I  B  E  O  L  Z  R  A  M  V  S  D
I  U  H  T  Y  M  O  N  O  R  E  T  U  E  D  A
R  S  E  G  E  N  E  S  I  S  J  I  N  L  A  R
A  E  R  A  M  O  S  B  R  E  V  O  R  P  N  Z
H  N  O  M  O  L  O  S  F  O  G  N  O  S  I  E
C  H  R  O  N  I  C  L  E  S  S  S  J  T  E  A
E  C  C  L  E  S  I  A  S  T  E  S  M  O  L  E
Z  E  P  H  A  N  I  A  H  K  I  N  G  S  B  N
H  A  I  A  S  I  A  G  G  A  H  A  N  O  J  T
```

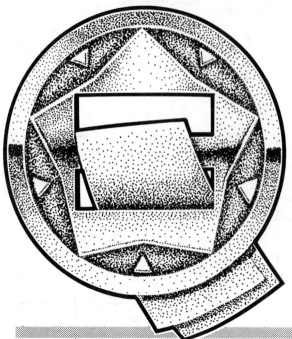

Quito's Shortwave Superpower

If you have a radio with good shortwave bands, you can pick up some of the world's "superpower" Christian stations—if you know exactly when and where to look for them. These stations virtually blanket the world with the gospel of Jesus Christ.

In Quito, Ecuador, for instance, radio HCJB has pioneered the field. It went on the air on Christmas Day in 1931, with a used 200-watt transmitter. Today its broadcasts go virtually around the world, and in 1981 it put a new 500,000-watt transmitter into service. (The government of Ecuador honored the station's fiftieth anniversary of broadcasting with a series of postage stamps.)

Other big operators in the field include Trans World Radio and the Far East Broadcasting Company. Their powerful signals all but cover the globe. Through their broadcasts millions have come to Jesus.

As an American listener, your best option is HCJB (short for Heralding Christ Jesus' Blessings). Though its main directional antennas beam toward the heart of South America and toward Europe, some of the HCJB signal spills over into the United States. Sometimes, too, shortwave signals, which bounce off the ionosphere, circle the globe. You can pick up the signal as it comes back!

Also, Quito's HCJB has more English programming than some of the other superpowers (nineteen hours a day), though your best time to pick it up is in the evening.

On the 19-meter band, you will find HCJB at 15.155. On the 31-meter band look for it at 9.745.

The Christian Kids Almanac recommends "The Passport Program," heard from 7:00 to 8:00 P.M. central standard time (adjust if you live in the East or West). In the summer, Ecuador remains on standard time, so you will have to adjust for that factor also. Just before "The Passport Program" is fifteen minutes of well-programmed international news. Enjoy also HCJB's music.

For the complete HCJB listening schedule, write: Voice of the Andes, HCJB, Box 3000, Opa Locka, Florida 33055.

Quizzing by Computer

This is the age of the computer, and now some kids are even finding ways to put home computers to "Christian" use.

Take Mark Entner, age fourteen, of Chicago Heights, Illinois. He's turned his computer into a "Bible quizzing machine."

With his own savings, Mark bought himself a Commodore Vic 20 keyboard for $178, then invested another $78 for the data set that went with it. Then he programmed it to help him and his church Bible quiz team rehearse the Book of Romans.

At his home, the quiz team gathers around Mark's keyboard for practice. Each one has his finger on a different key, ready to press quickly as soon as he recognizes the verse that Mark's dad is quoting from a stack of index cards.

No judge has to decide who pressed the button first. The computer calls it right every time.

If the contestant quotes the verse right, or completes a question correctly, Mark's dad informs the computer. If the answer is right, the computer also writes out "Yeaaaaaaaaa!" Three wrong answers, and the computer tells the contestant he's "frozen"—out of the game. Five right answers, and the contestant has "quizzed out," and someone else gets a chance.

In actual quizzing competition, contestants listen for key words to help them recall the verse. These are words that only appear once, or maybe twice, in the entire book chosen—in this case, Romans. The key words of Romans 1:14, for instance, would be those underlined: "I am *debtor* both to the *Greeks* and the *barbarians,* both to the *wise* and the *unwise.*"

Once a good quizzer hears the word *debtor,* he can usually identify the verse.

Mark's dad figured out a program to help the kids rehearse key words. With the help of a concordance, a man in Pennsylvania had already assembled all the key words of Romans into a book—just to help quiz teams. Mark and his dad programmed the Scriptures into the computer so these key words would stand out in red—to help the team identify them.

That's not all. For his church's annual missions conference, Mark may program a missions quiz. As people wander among the mission exhibits, they'll use the computer to test their knowledge of world missions.

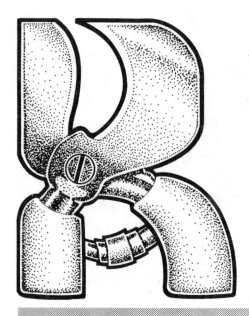

RadioWaves

In the past fifty years, God has raised up a number of extremely powerful shortwave stations that virtually blanket the world with the gospel of Jesus Christ.

One advantage of radio is that it can often go to regions where missionaries can't travel. Missionary radio penetrates into Communist and Muslim lands, triggering thousands of letters each month. And because of the nature of shortwave, which bounces off the ionosphere, its signal can also reach into remote jungle and mountain areas around the world.

The three largest mission organizations working in radio are the Far East Broadcasting Company, Trans World Radio, and World Radio Missionary Fellowship. These radio stations can tell hundreds of fascinating stories about their outreach, but here is one of the best:

Isolated tribespeople in Laos found a broadcast about God so fascinating that they wanted to know where to contact him. But how would they do so?

The address given on the broadcast was a post office box many miles of jungle trails away from them. Did God live in that box? Village elders sent three men to find out.

They found the box, bu no one was

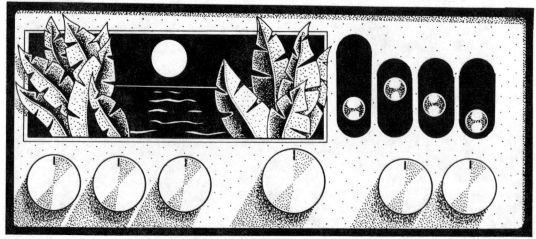

there. So they waited—for three days. Finally, they spotted a missionary opening the box.

They asked him if he was God.

"No," said the missionary, but he explained that he could help them know God.

The three tribal elders urgently insisted that the missionary follow them back to their village. Soon three thousand spirit worshipers found Jesus Christ. As they, too, spread the Word, the number of converts in this one little remote pocket of Laos grew to forty-five thousand!

It could not have happened without shortwave radio.

Dr. Louis Muggleton, a Christian physicist, holds his Ph.D. in antennas and radio propagation—the science of how radio waves travel. As part of his research, he has mapped the entire ionosphere worldwide. After years of study, he has concluded that there is no known function for the ionosphere other than reflecting radio waves.

Could it be that God constructed those reflecting layers at the creation of the world as part of his strategy for gospel outreach in this century?

When you're thinking about careers, you might want to keep radio missions in mind. They employ a wide variety of people— from speakers to musicians to broadcast engineers!

(For more on Christian radio, see *Hams* and *Quito's Shortwave Superpower.*)

Railroad Church

In the early days of this century, in small country towns along a railroad, kids might suddenly run to tell their parents, "A church just pulled into town!"

The church they referred to was a railroad "chapel car." When homesteaders migrated west in the 1800s, they often left their churches behind. The chapel car brought church and Sunday school to many of those in tiny towns where there was no church. It also carried library books and magazines.

Half of the car would be fixed up like a church, with a pulpit, organ, pews, and enough room to handle 80 adults and up to 150 Sunday school kids. The other part of the car was made into a home for the traveling minister, or missionary, and his family.

The railroad might detach the car on a siding and leave it in an area for several days, weeks, or even months. People would come to the chapel from far and near, in wagons, on horseback, and on foot.

These chapels on wheels might have been fun for the kids who got to visit them, but those who lived in them thought differently. Every time the car was switched to a sidetrack, which was often once or twice daily, everything in the refrigerator got jumbled up. "Milk, potatoes, jelly—all together!" wrote one missionary.

Originally there were seven chapel cars. Today one is on display at Green Lake, Wisconsin, and the oldest one still in existence can be seen at the museum of Prairie Village, near Madison, South Dakota.

Chapel Car Grace is a museum today.

Ranches

The gates of the rodeo chute open. A twisting bull charges headlong into the arena and jolts the cowboy on his back. Kids in the stands scream and cheer. When the rider bites the dust, a rodeo clown rushes in to distract the bull in another direction.

There's action like this every summer at River Valley Ranch, just one of many Christian ranches available to kids who love horses and the life of the Old West. Here are several *The Christian Kids Almanac* recommends, in the East, Midwest, and West:

River Valley Ranch. This is where buffalo roam, lanky cowboys tromp the board walkway of Main Street, and a fifteen-passenger Concord stagecoach still travels a dusty dirt road of the past.

Must be somewhere in Wyoming, Colorado, or Arizona—right?

Wrong. You're more than two thousand miles off the trail! River Valley Ranch is in hill country of north central Maryland, some fifty miles up from Baltimore.

There, in Gunpowder Valley, all the glamour and romance of the Old West locks arms with the metropolitan East. In spite of the unlikely location, these ranch hands know their business. (See *Nevada Steve*.)

For information, write: River Valley Ranch, Route 1, Millers, Maryland 21107.

Silver Birch Ranch. Located on Sawyer Lake near the wild Wolf River in Wisconsin's Nicolet National Forest, this ranch has hundreds of miles of trails for horseback riders, hikers, and skiers. It also features canoeing, rafting, team sports, and much more. Boys and girls eight years old and up can get in on the Silver Birch

Ranch's year-round program, and so can parents. Write: Silver Birch Ranch, White Lake, Wisconsin 54491.

Circle C Ranch. Top-ranking rodeo performers hold rodeo clinics here for young people, and this North Dakota ranch is also tops in teaching horsemanship. "Cowtown," a street right out of the Old West, rises next to the rodeo arena.

But you don't really know the Circle C Ranch until you meet Trish Lenihan, the ranch director. She is both a singer and a rodeo performer, and she grew up on this ranch when it was the Lenihan Hereford Ranch.

The Circle C Ranch brand looks like this: ©. It means that Christ is at the center of all that happens there.

Write: Circle C Ranch, P.O. Box 2401, Bismarck, North Dakota 58502.

Singin' River Ranch. This ranch sponsors adventure camps for boys and girls ages nine to seventeen, June through August. There you can ride horses, backpack, and shoot the river rapids. The ranch program stresses horsemanship, but also has sports, archery, crafts, and much more. Write: Singin' River Ranch, Route 5, Box 454, Evergreen, Colorado 80439.

Clydehurst Christian Ranch. Camps for kids start at age nine, and there's a great program for parents, too. Total ranch capacity is one thousand, and the setting is the beautiful Gallatin National Forest. Write: Clydehurst Christian Ranch, 802 North Twenty-Seventh Street, Billings, Montana 59101.

Frontier Ranch. This fantastic ranch in central Colorado, operated by Young Life, is especially geared to teens who are involved in the Young Life club movement. Parents can stay at Young Life's beautiful Trail West Lodge, only twenty minutes away. Write Young Life, P.O. Box KK, Buena Vista, Colorado 81211.

Rocky Mountain Lodge and Outfitters. Just four miles outside Grand Teton National Park in Wyoming, this ranch specializes in hosting youth groups. (See *Grand Teton Trail-trekkers* for more information.)

Red Sea Parts Again?

Four thousand years ago, as the Egyptian army thundered in hot pursuit, God parted the Red Sea so that Moses and the Israelites could escape.

No one can really duplicate this great event in history, of course, but in filming *The Ten Commandments,* Universal Studios of Hollywood gave it a good try.

In a tour of the studios, they like to show you how their equipment parted a lake 600 feet long, 150 feet wide, and 5 feet deep (enough, say filmmakers, to create the proper effect). The tram that takes you around on a tour of the studios waits for the water to part, then drives through. The waters close in behind you promptly.

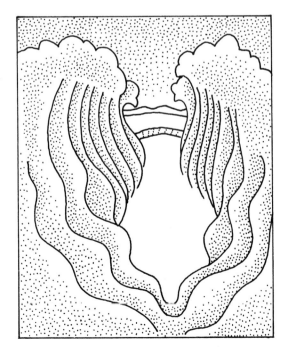

Refugees

You probably realize that many of the world's people are uprooted from their homes because of hunger, disease, war, or political persecution. They're called refugees. You may even have some refugee children in your school.

Can you guess how many refugees there are in the world? The United Nations estimates that there are ten million, some on every continent—and over half of them are women and children.

Happily, many Christian groups are involved in helping some of these refugees, and in resettling them in the United States. You can help out, too.

World Relief, a Christian organization, is one of twelve agencies authorized by the government to help refugees find homes in the United States. World Relief, however, wants to do more than finding homes. The organization also tries to find sponsors—churches and families—who will help take care of the refugees until they learn how to live here on their own.

Here are some suggestions from World Relief on ways you can help refugees feel at home here. Some of these apply to refugees just arriving on a plane; others can apply to children you may already know at church or at school.

- Help find clothes for refugees. Many leave their own homes with nothing but the clothes on their backs—and those might not be suited to the American climate.
- Help make their new homes ready for them by cleaning before they move in.
- Talk with them. Talking with friends will help their English skills improve.
- If you can baby-sit, offer to watch any young children for free while parents attend English classes or job training classes.
- Show them how to use public transportation.
- Participate in book drives to provide material to increase their reading skills.
- Host parties where they can meet other Americans.
- Involve them in youth activities at church.
- Help school kids with their homework.

If you'd like to help refugees in your area, but don't know how or where, you can volunteer your time through a local World Relief office. Call their toll-free number: (800) 431-2808. (New Yorkers call 914-268-4135.)

Or you might also want to ask your pastor about any other Christian groups working with refugees, perhaps from your denomination.

Rhode Island

Though many of America's first settlers came here to escape religious persecution, no American colony offered complete religious toleration until 1636. That colony was Rhode Island, founded by the courageous Roger Williams.

Williams, a young minister, had come to the Massachusetts Bay Colony in 1631. But he soon found that he didn't agree with the way the government was run. The Puritans were unwilling to let anyone worship God in any way but their own. When Williams protested this matter and also Puritan treatment of the Indians, he was banished.

Fortunately, Williams had friends among the Indians. (He later studied their language and wrote a book about it.) The Narragansetts let him buy land to establish a new homesite. Williams called the settlement Providence, which, from its dictionary definition, suggests "the help of God." There people were allowed to worship however they pleased.

Williams also founded the first Baptist church in America, in Providence in 1638.

Religious freedom—freedom for all viewpoints, not just one—was later written into the United States Constitution. (See *Bill of Rights.*)

FREE: Rhode Island Map

Learn more about the state founded by Roger Williams. Send for a colorful brochure and free road map of Rhode Island. Write: Department of Economic Development, Tourist Promotion, 1 Weybosset Hill, Providence, Rhode Island 02903.

Riddles

Q. Where could the Israelites have deposited their money?
A. *At the banks of the Jordan.*

Q. How do we know Peter was a rich fisherman?
A. *By his net income.*

Q. In what room of the Persian king's house did Daniel spend the night?
A. *In the den.*

Q. How do we know Samson was a great actor?
A. *He brought the house down.*

These riddles, and dozens more, were all written or collected by Myra Shofner for her popular *Ark Book of Riddles* and *Second Ark Book of Riddles*, both published by David C. Cook. Mrs. Shofner, a pastor's wife from Pensacola, Florida, sold her first manuscript (a poem) to a publisher at age thirteen.

In writing her Bible riddles, Shofner says she was "probably the first woman to read all the way through *Young's Analytical Concordance to the Bible.*" (She used the huge volume to get ideas for the puns and wordplay most of her riddles are based on.) Though the results are funny, the concordance wasn't much fun to read. Shofner says that it "changed the subject a little too often and had far too many characters!"

Robinson Crusoe

The book *Robinson Crusoe,* written in 1719 by Daniel Defoe, has been called "the greatest book of all time" and "the beginning of the modern novel."

Though today's readers might only barely detect it, the original unabridged version of *Robinson Crusoe* had a good deal of Christian content. Stranded on an island, the sailor Crusoe saw God work in his life. He accepted Jesus as his Savior, looked to God in hardship, and even attempted to bring his man Friday (a native whom he rescued from cannibals) to faith in Christ.

But in the making of many abridgments, the religious sections of the novel have now been almost entirely eliminated. Older, less abridged editions may be available in some libraries, however.

Rodeo Cowboys

It takes a rugged man or woman to win in the rodeo arena. It also takes a lot of skill. Whether it's bronc riding, bull riding, steer wrestling, or calf roping you compete in, you've got to spend hours of practice.

Unfortunately, for many years the professional rodeo circuit had many fine riders, but few cowboys who cared at all about spiritual things, or who dared to speak openly about the Lord. (One exception over the years was a highly respected rodeo clown by the name of Wilbur Plaugher. Rodeo clowns are more than clowns—they're in the arena to distract raging bulls and save lives.) Something had to change.

The first big break came in 1974, at the famous Frontier Days Rodeo in Cheyenne, Wyoming. A handful of Christian cowboys there decided to hold a public service and invite their rodeo friends. They were afraid only a few would show up. But three hundred turned out! Several men stood up and told how Jesus had changed their lives. Others came to believe in the Lord that day. Shortly afterward, the Christians formed a cowboy chapter of the Fellowship of Christian Athletes (FCA).

One of the men God used in the breakthrough was Mark Schricker, the first cowboy ever to win two events at the National Rodeo Finals, and runner-up to three all-around world champions. Larry Mahan, Dean Oliver, Bob Ragsdale—he has competed against them all.

The other man was rodeo clown Wilbur Plaugher.

Now Christian cowboys are giving rodeo a new image, according to Plaugher. "Who would ever dream of the change in the image of the cowboy? The old-timers thought rodeo was a place to go to drink and tear up hotels. I remember when the hotels in Houston, Texas, wouldn't even let you in if you had a big hat," he says.

Already the Christian cowboys have published two volumes of magazine-style testimonial books, with the conversion stories of more than sixty professional rodeo performers. They distributed or sold fifteen thousand copies of the first edition! They are out to influence not only rodeo cowboys, but ranchers, cattlemen, and others in the livestock business. And they're beginning to make an impact among teens and at "Little Britches" and amateur rodeos.

Any young person can join the cowboy chapter of the FCA for just $7.00 a year. When you join, they will send you a membership packet that includes a Cowboy Bible, bumper stickers, window decals, and a monthly newsletter called *Circuit Rider.*

Mail your request for membership to: Cowboy Chapter, FCA, P.O. Box 56, Coal Creek, Colorado 81221.

Dave Brock ropes calves—and shares his faith, too.

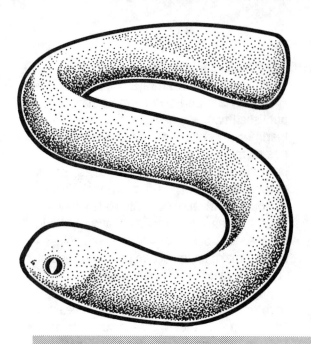

Sahara Adventure

Several years ago an American by the name of Dick Ewing went with four friends to try to ride motorcycles thirty-five hundred miles across the Sahara Desert. Why? Because it had never been done before.

The going proved incredibly difficult. One man gave up after 380 miles, but the other four pressed on. Then, seven hundred miles into the desert, all their reserve gas spilled into the sand when a rack broke. The outlook seemed hopeless.

Though Ewing was not a Christian, he was desperate, and decided to pray. Afterward, the men looked up and saw an Algerian Army truck that had come seemingly from out of nowhere. The soldiers gave them fuel and water.

"How often does this truck pass through here?" the cyclists inquired.

"About every sixty days," was the answer.

Twelve hundred miles into the desert—in the remotest part—the four men lost all their water in another accident. The next well on their map was ninety-five miles away. Death seemed certain.

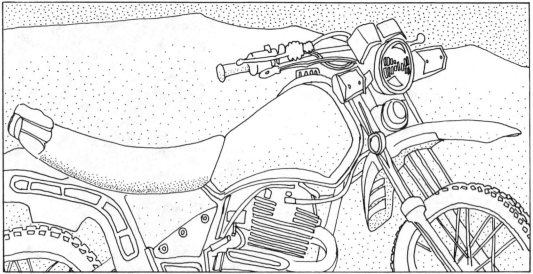

Again, Ewing prayed.

The men had brought a packet of forty-two detailed aerial photographic maps of the desert, but had dumped them earlier to lighten their load. Yet one man felt compelled to look in his pack. He found one map left. It was the map of the very area they were in! And it showed a well only five miles away.

In a third catastrophe, Ewing's motorcycle hit some rocks. All 350 pounds came down on top of him. His leg appeared broken, with no help in sight. Again, death appeared certain.

Ewing, who had been reading a pocket Bible given to him by his girl friend, saw the mess he had made of his life. He wanted to be ready to face death. Then and there, in the middle of the burning desert, he accepted Jesus as his Savior.

Then, once more, Ewing prayed for help.

He looked up to see a truck in the distance coming straight toward them! The truck took the men to a dispensary at a desert oasis.

Ewing eventually finished the desert trek. Since he also took film footage of the experience, you can see it in the movie *Ultimate Adventure*, produced by the Moody Institute of Science.

What is Ewing doing today?

For the last several years he has been traveling in the U.S. and abroad, showing this remarkable film about four daring but foolish men who tried to cross the Sahara on "iron camels." Then he invites his audiences to what he calls the "ultimate adventure": a life with Jesus Christ as Lord.

Saint Patrick

If you live near Chicago, you know St. Patrick's Day as the day the city dyes the Chicago River green. Really! Irish people all over the world wear shamrocks and celebrate on March 17.

But who was the real Patrick?

At the beginning of the fifth century A.D., pirates kidnapped sixteen-year-old Patrick Succat from his father's villa on the west coast of England and took him to Ireland. There they put him to work tending the cattle of an Irish chieftain.

In his poverty and loneliness, Patrick turned to Christ for the forgiveness of his sins, and spent much of his day praying.

After six years, he escaped and found his way back to his family. But, amazingly, he returned to Ireland several years later to preach the gospel in the land of his captors.

Patrick preached in Ireland for many years, and founded some three hundred Christian churches there. After his death, Irish Christians, many of them converts from Patrick's preaching, spread their faith to other parts of Europe. The first missionary to Scotland came from Ireland.

Legend has it that Patrick used the Irish shamrock to explain the Trinity. It has one stem and three leaves, just as our one God is also three persons—Father, Son, and Holy Spirit.

When next March 17 comes around, and many of your friends are wearing green, remember the real Patrick, a young missionary of God's love.

Science Films

Are science classes some of your favorites at school? Then you'll be glad to hear about the surprising number of science films available that acknowledge God as the Creator of the universe that science studies. Here are a number of these films that *The Christian Kids Almanac* recommends. Your church or club may want to order some.

City of the Bees (Moody Institute of Science). This surprising film tells about beehive cities that boast air conditioning, police and sanitation squads, nurseries, chemical processing plants, some remarkable structural engineers, and a concise language that man has learned to "read."

Dust or Destiny (Moody Institute of Science). Here you meet fish that lay eggs on dry land, birds that migrate for thousands of miles without map or compass, and bats that fly through total darkness without the slightest chance of collision.

Energy in a Twilight World (Moody Institute of Science). One of the newest films, this one explores our energy resources, and how, as Christians, we should handle them. For instance, with just six percent of the world's population, the United States owns half of all automobiles, uses half of the world's gasoline, and conducts half of the world's air travel!

Footprints in Stone (Films for Christ). This film challenges the idea that dinosaurs disappeared long ago before man appeared on the earth. For impressive evidence, it takes you to the Paluxy River bed of Texas to show you human footprints in the same rock stratum with dinosaur tracks. A sequel to *The Great Dinosaur Mystery.*

God of Creation (Moody Institute of Sci-

In Footprints in Stone, *you can examine dinosaur tracks in Texas.*

Photo courtesy of Films for Christ

Dust or Destiny *shows you fish on land!* ▶

ence). With the telescope this popular film explores the immensity of space, and with the microscope it peers into the unseen world—like the teeming world of tiny creatures found in a single drop of water.

The Great Dinosaur Mystery (Films for Christ). Dinosaurs seem to capture the fancy of both young and old. But almost every dinosaur book one picks up says these creatures lived millions of years ago—long before man evolved on the earth.

This seems to contradict the Bible. But wait a minute. Are dinosaurs really that old? This film says no, and sets out to show you the evidence.

Origins—How the World Came to Be (Films for Christ). Dramatic evidence of the Earth's original divine creation, and devastating evidence against the standard theory of evolution. This is actually a series of six powerful thirty-minute films, released in

1982 in cooperation with the California-based Institute for Creation Research.

Time and Eternity (Moody Institute of Science). Explains the meaning of space and time. An imaginary "time microscope" magnifies a split second for you, and a "time compressor" squeezes days and weeks into minutes. The confusing results of traveling near the speed of light are also explored.

Voice of the Deep (Moody Institute of Science). This film takes you on a trip beneath the sea. You will see the beauty of the undersea world, and hear fish that croak, shrimp that clack, porpoises that moo, and a din of other mysterious noises.

The World That Perished (Films for Christ). This film is an account of Noah's ark and the flood as recorded in Genesis. Only eight people, it reminds us, survived the most awesome catastrophe this planet has ever known.

Shroud of Turin

In recent years, the Shroud of Turin has received worldwide attention. It is a piece of cloth from a cathedral in Turin, Italy. But some believe it to be the actual burial cloth of Jesus Christ, for it bears the image of a crucified man.

Perhaps you have seen a documentary about this shroud on tv, or read about it in a magazine or newspaper. Could it really be Christ's shroud, or is it a forgery of some kind? Let's examine some of the evidence.

With the naked eye, one can faintly see on the cloth the image of a man. Close study shows that he has been scourged and beaten. Nails have been driven through both wrists and one spike through both feet.

Bloodstains on the cloth reveal numerous wounds.

There is a deep wound in the man's side, and puncture wounds about his head.

But something else sets this piece of cloth entirely apart from other church relics of the past—and there have been many.

A man named Secondo Pia made the discovery in 1898, when the Roman Catholic Church authorized him to take the first official photograph of the shroud.

When the film was developed, he was speechless. The negative photographic plate showed a positive image. Impossible! This would violate all the rules of photography!

You know that if you take a snapshot of a white house against a dark sky, then examine the negative that your photo processor sends back, the house will be black, and the sky light. That's what a negative is— just the opposite of the final print itself.

If the white house showed white on the negative, there would be something terribly wrong. For that would give you a black house in the actual print!

Obviously, there was something very un-usual about the Shroud of Turin.

Not long ago a team of expert scientists examined the shroud—among them nuclear physicists, laser technicians, chemists, and engineers. With the latest scientific equipment they put the cloth through all kinds of tests.

When processed through a machine at the Jet Propulsion Lab in Pasadena, California, analysts were able to determine that two soldiers, using different lashes, had scourged the victim. One had lashed from the left side, the other from the right.

One team fed the shroud photographs into a computer used to analyze photos

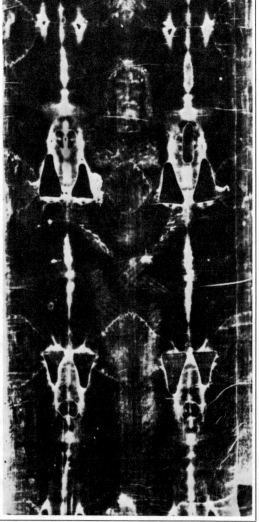

taken from space. Its findings were also startling. The image came back three-dimensional!

Critics of the shroud have tried to write it off as a hoax. But evidence mounts that this piece of cloth cannot be so lightly dismissed. It would be impossible for someone to forge the image on it, scientists say, especially with the tools of the Middle Ages. Chemists say the cloth may have been scorched, as if subjected by the corpse to a burst of radiant energy.

How could this have happened?

Steve Lawhead, who wrote an intriguing report on the shroud for *Campus Life* magazine, suggests that the Bible may give us the best clue. And so he writes this descriptive narrative:

The garden is quiet; the night passed uneventfully. Pilate's soldiers are standing guard over the entrance to the rock tomb. One of them yawns; it will soon be dawn. They can see the sky growing gray in the east.

Inside the tomb all is dark and silent. In one blinding instant the black recesses of the tomb are suddenly alive with light. Dazzling, brilliant, living light. The earth shakes from the pent-up force and the heavy stone sealing the entrance to the tomb is rolled away. It's over instantaneously. The tomb is dark and silent once again, but changed.

Jesus is gone, and on the slab where he was laid—the empty shroud.

Shroud Replica

In Park Forest, Illinois, sixteen-year-old Michael McDonnell became so fascinated with the Shroud of Turin that he made a replica of it for an honors history course.

Michael purchased muslin at a fabric store. He soaked the muslin in lemon juice and olive oil, and then baked the cloth for about five hours in the kitchen oven at 160 degrees to give the material the appearance of great age.

Then, with his mother and a friend, he took it to the backyard and burned holes in the cloth with a candle (the real shroud had been scorched in a fire).

After that, using pastel oils in shades of tan, Michael spent about three hours reproducing the image of the crucified man on the cloth.

The replica was exhibited at a school history fair, and Michael stood by to answer questions of the curious. "A lot of people who looked at the project went away wondering, and that was what I wanted," he said.

Although Michael is fully convinced that

Jesus Christ rose from the dead, he admits that the existence of the shroud is not proof in itself, merely circumstantial evidence. "You have to have faith," he says.

The project earned Michael an *A* in the history course.

Sign of Love

How would you tell a deaf or hearing-impaired friend that God loves him (or impaired friend that God loves him (or her)? It's easy. In the sequence below, Kelly Singer of Wheaton, Illinois, shows you how.

"Snowflake" Bentley

You may have heard this fact in school: No two snowflakes are alike. Each one that falls has its own design. And the one who discovered this was "Snowflake" Bentley.

Willie Bentley lived in the hills of Vermont about a century ago. He was curious about everything in the world around him—a natural scientist, it seemed.

When he acquired a microscope as a he drew three hundred of them. Why? "Since no two are alike," he explained, "when one melts, its beautiful design is gone." Sketching preserved those designs.

But sketching was so slow. Then in a catalog Willie found his answer—a camera that would photograph into a microscope. Remember, this was nearly a century ago!

On January 15, 1885, while still a teenager, Bentley entered these words in his brown notebook: "First snow crystals ever photomicrographed."

The scientific world didn't know Bentley

young teen, the excited Bentley soon discovered a whole new world. He examined a rose petal, a blade of grass, a crow's feather, insects, and wild flowers.

It was during a thunderstorm one night, as he watched out his bedroom window, that Willie decided he wanted to study water most of all—water in all its forms. That meant rain, hail, ice, and snow.

That's how he discovered that no two designs of a snowflake are alike.

Willie set himself up in a barn and began to sketch snowflakes. Over three winters until a Vermont geology professor learned about his patient research. Though he never attended a university, in time Bentley became known throughout the U.S. Weather Bureau. He was the first scientist to accurately measure raindrops and determine how and why they were the size they were. Before his death he was recognized by scientists in the United States and abroad.

His interest in snowflakes never wavered. Between the ages of nineteen and sixty-six, Snowflake Bentley made some 5,381 photomicrographs! The best were published recently in a book, for their scientific detail and, as Bentley himself said, for "the beauty that God has placed in each individual snowflake." For Bentley was a Christian, and knew who had created the world he studied.

"If you have a dream and a talent," Bentley told young people before he died, "make the most of it. The whole world is there for you to discover."

Soccer, American Style

Soccer has long been the world's number one sport, played in 142 countries—more than there are in the United Nations. But only in recent years has it caught on in the United States. In 1982 it became America's most popular youth sports activity.

Some of America's best soccer players, by the way, are "missionary kids" (MKs). That's because they grew up on the foreign mission field and learned the game early in life.

One of the nation's newest and most unusual professional soccer teams is the Memphis Americans.

In 1981 a group of Christians bought what had been the Hartford, Connecticut "Hellions," and moved the franchise to Memphis. They saw soccer as a means to reach a city and its youth with clear Christian values. The owners, front office staff, general manager, coaches, and a number of the players are Christians. Several have served with Campus Crusade's Athletes in Action. Their vice-president is Kyle Rote, Jr., one of the great soccer players of all time, who recently retired from play. Kyle is the only native American ever to win the North American Soccer League scoring championship.

The son of Kyle Rote, Sr., the former all-pro football star with the New York Giants, young Kyle turned down a lucrative NFL contract to play soccer for a very meager salary with the Dallas Tornado. But in so doing, he helped "put soccer on the map" in the United States. Even more important,

soccer has given this superstar a world platform for sharing the gospel.

"Through soccer, played as it is in every country," says Rote, "a person could actually reach the whole world."

Besides playing the game, Kyle Rote's Memphis Americans also run the American Soccer Academy for boys and girls ages five to eighteen, one of the best in the nation. There young players are taught the basic skills of the game, such as dribbling, passing, shooting, and heading. The instructors are all Christians, and each class includes a ten-minute talk from the Bible.

Photo courtesy of the Memphis Americans

Softball Speed Queen

The pitcher who is the subject of this article has:

• pitched against Willie Mays and Johnny Bench.

• struck out three out of four New York Mets in an exhibition game in 1974—the same year they won the World Series.

• posted, in seventeen years of pitching, nearly 40,000 strikeouts, over 250 perfect games, over 750 shutouts, and nearly 600 no-hitters.

Who is this person? The winner of a Cy Young award? The hottest pitcher in pro baseball?

No. She's a softball pitcher named Rosie Black, and around the ball diamond they call her "the Queen." Her powerful pitch travels nearly 100 miles per hour. With her team of two outfielders and a catcher, called "The Queen and Her Court," Rosie plays exhibition games all over the world—and wins! She has appeared on the nation's top talk shows, on "Kids Are People, Too," and on "That's Incredible."

Rosie started her remarkable career as a kid. She was just ten years old when she tried out for shortstop in a Los Angeles girls' park league. But first everyone had to try for the pitching position. When Rosie went to the mound, she gave the batter a "windmill windup," like she'd seen her dad do in the men's leagues. Those looking on were impressed.

Rosie's dad soon realized her talent, and taught her how to grip the ball and throw it properly. "It's important," she says, "that you learn the right habits from the start."

Her dad soon assembled a kids' championship softball team at California's Rolling Hills Estates, where "The Queen and Her Court" is still based. With Rosie's amazing speed, they won every game in sight.

There was just one problem. What kid could catch for Rosie, with her phenomenal speed? Only one could—her eight-year-old sister, Eileen! What a pair they made!

One of the spectators said one day, "Boy, with that pitcher and catcher, who needs a team?"

And that's when they decided to take on their opponents with only four people. Out of this idea came "The Queen and Her Court."

Today Rosie is thirty years old, but she's still pitching. Eileen catches. Rosie's husband, Paul, covers all the outfield left of center. He's a near world-record sprinter, and a powerhouse hitter who can easily slam balls over the fence.

Rosie's brother Norman, a six-foot, curly-haired, strawberry blond nicknamed, "Lotta Chatter," covers right field and provides team comedy. He can throw three balls at one time—accurately.

Rosie will often strike out her batter blindfolded! Her pitches include fastballs, curves, risers, drops, knuckleballs, and change-ups.

Not long ago, her team won four games straight against Japan's major league baseball stars in the Tokyo Giants Stadium. Thirty million people watched each of the four telecasts.

Rosie Black is a strong Christian, as are the other members of her team. She came to Christ at age ten, the same year she started pitching. Now at every game, she gives a testimony over the microphone. Only once over the years has she heard someone catcall because of her stand for Jesus.

Rosie and her family are convinced that God has given them their sports talents. Why? Perhaps so they could tell the world about Jesus.

And that's exactly what they are doing.

Sound of Music

The Sound of Music turned out to be one of the stage and screen successes of our century. Rebellious Maria, orphaned as a child, leaves a convent to work for Baron Georg von Trapp as a governess to his seven children, whose mother has died.

She settles in at the massive von Trapp villa against the mountains at Salzburg, and her working relationship blooms into love and marriage. But when the baron, a former admiral in the Austrian navy, is summoned to join Hitler's navy, he balks. As the Nazi pressure builds, the von Trapps flee by night over the mountains to Italy and their freedom. They choose to leave their valuable estate and almost all their belongings behind to save their political freedom and spiritual integrity.

In the screen version, Julie Andrews plays the role of Maria. But what happened to the real Maria?

The real Maria von Trapp, who has written a number of books for the evangelical Christian market, lives in Vermont.

In her books she tells some of the true story of her life: her being sent from the convent to care for the von Trapp children, the growing love between her and Georg von Trapp, and the start of the von Trapp Family Singers. Some events were "condensed" for the musical and film, *The Sound of Music.* For example, the family had already sung all over Europe before they decided to flee Austria, and this made their travel easier. Also, Maria and Georg had already had a child of their own before they left! Shortly after they fled their home, they settled in America with their children—who soon numbered nine!

Maria still helps to host travelers today at the Trapp Family Lodge near the resort village of Stowe. A fire just before Christmas of 1980 destroyed the main lodge and some of Maria's priceless belongings ("favorite things"), but a new building opened in the winter of 1981-82. Nearly eight thousand people attended the lodge's "Open House" on that occasion!

The Von Trapps pose in Vermont in the 1940s.

Photo courtesy of the Trapp Family Lodge

Space Shuttle

On March 29, 1982, the *Columbia* space shuttle, commanded by astronaut Jack Lousma, circled the earth, unable to come down. Rains had soaked the scheduled California landing site, and drifting sand from ravaging winds had closed the runway at the backup landing site in New Mexico. Ominous newspaper headlines read: "Delayed Shuttle Looking for a Way to Come Home."

The next day, fortunately, the winds abated, and Houston Control gave its OK to land in New Mexico. Colonel Lousma, orbiting at four miles per second, began his descent and gradually slowed his craft. Yet he was still going sixteen times the speed of sound over Los Angeles!

At such speeds it might seem impossible to land on target. But Lousma, in a beautiful descent watched by millions on television, brought *Columbia* in to a perfect landing, stopping his craft just at the runway's marker line. Millions watching cheered.

Lousma deserves at least part of the credit for the landing, but he is also quick to explain the spacecraft's remarkable guidance system. It contains what is called a "reference trajectory," or computerized plan of flight. Computers monitor the actual flight, second by second, to make sure the spacecraft is following the plan. If not, they make corrections.

If for some reason, however, some part of the guidance system doesn't "hear" all the signals, or fails to follow them, the spacecraft could be headed off course toward potential disaster.

Colonel Lousma, who received Jesus Christ as his Savior as a boy, reminds listeners today that God also has a plan, or course, for each of their lives. By keeping in close contact with God, you can be sure that your life will proceed on the best course.

(For another story about Colonel Lousma, see *Football Prayer*.)

SEND FOR: Space Shuttle Model

Here's an opportunity to send up your own space shuttle from your backyard. You can purchase an authentic model of the Rockwell International Space Shuttle Orbiter, made of laminated styrene and balsa wood. It snaps together easily. Launch it by hand. Facts about the real space shuttle are included.

To obtain your Tiger Squadron Space Shuttle Orbiter, send $1.85 plus 50¢ for postage and handling to the Hayden Planetarium Shop, 81st Street and Central Park West, New York, New York 10024. (New York State residents add 15¢ tax.)

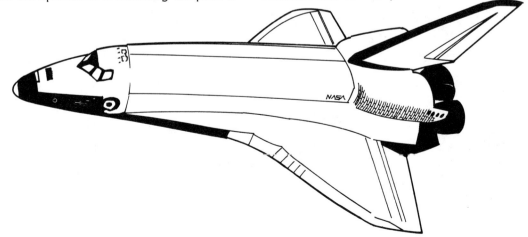

Sports Films

In the past few years, the Christian film industry has produced a number of exciting films on Christian athletes. As a kid, you won't have the money to go out and rent one of these on your own, but your church might want to do so.

Beyond Victory (New Liberty Films). This film's Olympic competition footage includes 1976 gold medalist John Naber (swimming), Maxie Parks (track), John Peterson (wrestling). Also appearing are all-pro football lineman Rich Saul, basketball's Paul Westphal, soccer's Derek Smethurst, and quarterback Jim Zorn of the Seattle Seahawks.

The Devil's Coach (Outreach Films). This film tells the stormy story of Jim Brock, baseball coach of the top-ranked Arizona State University Sun Devils.

Football Fever (Omega Films). Unfolds with outrageous football comedy, National Football League gridiron action, and in-depth inspirational interviews with some of the best players of the NFL.

The Last Out (Glenray). Ten-year-old Jose idolizes professional baseball players and dreams of the day he can join their ranks. "Little Leaguer Wilbur" can't catch, throw, or slide, but Jose learns a valuable lesson from him about forgiveness and friendship. A sports film especially for kids.

More Than Winning (Life Productions). This sports documentary features Tom Landry, Bobby Jones, Ed Kea, Pat Kelly, and Kyle Rote, Jr. Narrated by Bobby Richardson, former New York Yankee.

The Prize (Outreach Films). The high-energy world of "free-style" skiing provides the setting for the story of skier Rick Jenkins.

Soccer Fever (Omega Films). Featuring Christian soccer pros from countries around the world, this movie was filmed in part at the 1982 World Cup games in Spain. It also includes a short dramatic sequence about a South American boy who grows up to become a world champion.

Sports Capers (Omega Films). This hilarious film is a medley of sports bloopers, exciting action, and comedy in scenes from many different sports. A number of pro athletes also share their faith.

Sports Galaxy (Omega Films). This film

Photo courtesy of Dave Singer

vividly displays the excitement of skydiving, ski flying, and hot-air ballooning. It also includes comedy, scenes from early aviation, and space flight.

A Sports Odyssey (Omega Films). This unusual sports film includes scenes of surfing, ski jumping, hang gliding, and skateboarding. At the close, several Christian champions testify of their faith in Jesus Christ. An Emmy Award winner for Best Cinematography.

Superstars on Location (Gospel Films). This new film takes a look at some Christians in the world of professional athletics. The release features Tom Landry, Roger Staubach (now retired), Bob Breunig, John Stallworth, Donnie Shell, Raphael Septien, Mike Schmidt, Pat Kelly, and Gary Carter.

The Tommy John Story (Quadrus). The story of how a celebrated major league pitcher made his remarkable recovery from a devastating injury. Includes footage from National League play-off games as well as World Series action.

Your Body, His Temple (Ken Anderson Films). Stresses physical fitness from a Christian view. Features former Olympic medal winners Jim Ryun and Doris Brown-Heritage, along with marathon champions Jeff Wells and Chuck Smead.

Sporty Senior

Would you believe that the man doing a "muscle out" in the photo at right is 101 years old?

That's right. Thomas Edward Harper of Belleville, Illinois (known to friends as "Reverend Tommy") is in great shape. Though his sight and hearing have dimmed in recent years, the strict exercise program Rev. Harper has followed since 1919 has given him the strength not only for "muscle outs," but also for preaching and constructing churches.

Raised in a log cabin, Rev. Harper has been married for sixty-eight years, and has been a pastor and evangelist for over thirty. He especially enjoys working with children and young adults, and he is honorary chaplain of the United States Air Force. He preaches hundreds of times annually.

When he gets up each morning, Rev. Harper prays, "Lord, let me win someone to Jesus today."

And whenever anyone asks him what gives him his energy, Harper replies, "A clean life and a happy heart!"

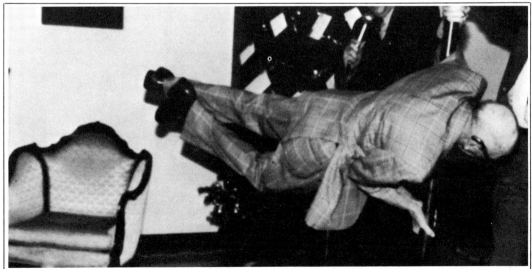

Stamp Collectors

Philatelists, or stamp collectors, come in all ages, for stamp collecting is an enjoyable hobby on many different levels. Postage stamps tell stories—about far places or people and events of the past.

Some philatelists like to collect stamps by topics: birds, wild animals, and so on. You can create your own topics. So why not start a mini-collection of stamps that, in some way, have a Christian theme?

Take the example of George Washington. Two U.S. stamps show him kneeling in prayer at Valley Forge. The first was released in 1928; a brighter and more exciting version followed in 1977.

You will find other stamps on many of the famous figures whose stories are touched upon in this book: William Penn, Noah Webster, Roger Williams, and Samuel Morse, to name a few.

Other stamps honor the Salvation Army, the *Apollo 15* moon mission (astronaut Jim Irwin on the moon rover), inventors, doctors, and presidents, some of whom were not ashamed to name Jesus Christ as their Savior.

Foreign missions might make a good collection theme. When the Auca Indians murdered five missionaries in the jungles of Ecuador a quarter century ago, Ecuador released a series of five stamps, one on each slain missionary. Stamps have been released honoring such powerful missionary radio stations as HCJB and the outreach of Trans World Radio.

Tom Budge, a Baptist minister and stamp collector in Australia, says, "There are not just dozens, or even hundreds, but thousands of different postage stamps from all over the world showing some aspect of Christianity or the Bible."

Budge has built up one of the largest collections of such stamps in existence. To-day he can illustrate the Bible from Genesis to Revelation with stamps. Stamp club talks have allowed him to share not only his expert knowledge of stamps, but also his faith in Christ.

It's easy to start your own stamp collection. You can buy stamp portfolios, by year, at your local post office. Look there also for the latest edition of *Stamps & Stories,* an inexpensive paperback catalog listing all United States stamps.

Star-Spangled Songwriter

On Chesapeake Bay the morning of September 14, 1814, Francis Scott Key peered anxiously through a pair of powerful field glasses, his eyes trying to pierce the morning mist and the lingering smoke of battle.

Key had been an overnight political prisoner of the British as they bombarded Baltimore's Fort McHenry. It was a fierce attack. Surely, thought Key, the fort must have fallen.

He squinted through the glasses one more time.

The flag was still there!

Shortly afterwards Key began to write—some say on the back of a letter or an envelope: "Oh, say, can you see, by the dawn's early light ... "

Not many Americans realize that five years after Key wrote what would later become the nation's national anthem, he wrote a hymn that is still in some Christian songbooks today:

"Lord, with glowing heart I'd praise Thee
For the bliss Thy love bestows,
For the pardoning grace that saves me,
And the peace that from it flows."

Francis Scott Key for a while considered becoming a minister. He helped found the American Sunday School Union, a movement which started thousands of Sunday schools across the nation in the 1800s, and served as its vice-president for some eighteen years.

Key understood clearly the spiritual foundations of the country he loved. If that nation should wander from God, he believed, it would soon be in trouble. This conviction he strongly implied in the last verse of "The Star-Spangled Banner": "And this be our motto: 'In God is our trust.' "

FREE: Star-Spangled Facts

Learn more about our flag and our national anthem. Read about Mary Pickersgill, the young woman who sewed the legendary flag that flew above Fort McHenry "in the rockets' red glare." Read more about Francis Scott Key, the Battle of Baltimore, and facts about our flag. For your free booklets and folders write: The Star-Spangled Banner Flag House, 844 East Pratt Street, Baltimore, Maryland 21202. Include twenty-five cents for postage and handling.

Stone Faces

We've all seen somber people with "stony expressions." But if you want to see some real stone faces, there are four places across the land where you can find them.

The most famous, of course, would have to be Mount Rushmore. Can you name the four presidents whose faces are embedded into the mountainside above the Black Hills of South Dakota? (Answer on next page.)

The sculptor here was French-born Gutzon Borglum. Yet it was hardly a job that could be done with a sculptor's standard techniques! It took the genius of engineers as well. Borglum designed a grouping of the four presidents to conform to the mountain's granite cap. But deep cracks and fissures later discovered in the rock required nine changes in the design.

Working from five-foot models for the four men, workmen had to transfer facial measurements, enlarged many times, to the mountainside. Once they positioned, say, the tip of a nose, they could begin to blast away the excess rock with dynamite. (They used 450,000 tons of the explosive in all.)

Drillers, suspended over the face of the mountain in "swing seats," used jackhammers to honeycomb the surface with shallow holes at intervals of about three inches. The remaining rock was wedged off with small drills, hammers, or wedging tools.

Stone Mountain honors the Confederacy.

Finally the sculpture was smoothed with a small air hammer in a process known as "bumping."

The project, known as the "Shrine of Democracy," took many years.

Abraham Lincoln is the only president facing a different direction than the others. Someone has noted that, while three of the presidents depicted came from families of wealth, Lincoln rose from the ranks of the poor.

Where are the other sets of stone faces?

Stone Mountain, Georgia, attracts millions each year. At this monument to the Confederacy, you can see three more famous figures of history carved on the mountainside. Can you name these also? (Answer on next page.) The project was completed in 1970.

You will find a third stone face in the mountains of New Hampshire, carved many thousands of years ago, not by man, but by

Nature carved "The Great Stone Face."

Photo courtesy of USDA Forest Service

nature. Some call this forty-foot granite profile the "old man of the mountains." Years ago Nathaniel Hawthorne gained immortality for the rock formation with his classic short story, "The Great Stone Face"—for which an editor named John Greenleaf Whittier paid him twenty-five dollars. Daniel Webster attributed the work to "God Almighty," who had "hung out a sign to show that there He makes men."

The world's largest man-made sculpture is still in process. It is the huge, 563-foot-high statue of the Sioux chief Crazy Horse, now being blasted out of the rocky face of Thunderbird Mountain in the Black Hills of South Dakota.

When completed, it will be the world's largest sculpture, ten times bigger than the presidential heads at nearby Mount Rushmore! It is said that four thousand men will be able to stand on the chief's extended arm, and a five-room house would fit inside his horse's flaring nostril.

Sculptor Korczak Ziolkowski and his associates had been working on the Crazy Horse project for thirty-five years before his recent death. But two of his sons are carrying it on, and the sculpture is now beginning to take significant form. Already it has attracted more than a million visitors a year.

Answers:

Mt. Rushmore faces: George Washington, Thomas Jefferson, Abraham Lincoln, and Theodore Roosevelt. Stone Mountain faces: Robert E. Lee, Stonewall Jackson, and Jefferson Davis.

Strongest Man

Former weight lifter Paul Anderson is still listed in the *Guinness Book of World Records* as the strongest man in the world.

For years he has continued to break records. In 1957 he lifted 6,270 pounds in a back lift in Toccoa, Georgia, a record which has never since been even approached.

His biographer asserts that Mr. Anderson "can outlift by thirty pounds per lift the amateurs and Olympians you may see on television or read about in sports pages. They may be referred to as the strongest, but that's only because Paul Anderson no longer competes as an amateur."

The five-foot nine-inch, 375-pound Anderson has been an outspoken Christian for years. He could be making a big salary if he promoted himself, but he spends his energies instead on behalf of the two schools for needy boys that he established years ago in Georgia and Texas.

And he probably speaks to more high school students face-to-face than any other man in North America. At each engagement—up to five hundred a year—he

wows the audience with feats of strength, and then drives home his message.

"If getting to heaven were a contest, I'd lose," he booms, in a voice that needs no microphone. "But God loved me and saved me in spite of myself."

Another "strong" Christian is Jon Cole of Arizona, who has broken records in both Olympic and power lifts. Jon is probably best known for his pioneer work in weight training for sports, done with Arizona State University athletes.

Sunday, Billy

In the early part of this century, the most famous evangelist on the scene was not Billy Graham, but a former major league baseball pitcher named Billy Sunday. (That was his real name, too!)

Sunday pitched for the old Chicago White Stockings. (The name changed to Chicago White Sox in 1911.) Fans labeled him the only man who could round the diamond, touching every base, in fourteen seconds.

Sunday later left pro ball to become a full-time evangelist, though his pitching style carried over into his preaching. It was not unusual for him to go into a sort of windup, with one foot in the air, before delivering a rapid-fire sermon that had all the speed of a fastball!

His preaching was much more down-to-earth than the flowery sermons that people of his day were used to. When criticized, he commented, "I'm preaching for the age in which I live. If the English language gets in my way, I tramp all over it." Here are a few other colorful lines of his:

- Don't look as if your religion hurts you.
- I'm against sin. I'll kick it as long as I've got a foot, and I'll fight it as long as I've got a fist—I'll bite it as long as I've got a tooth. And when I'm old and fistless and footless and toothless, I'll gum it till I go home to heaven and it goes home to hell.
- The auto is not responsible for the falling off in church attendance. That fool thing will stand in the middle of the road until you tell it where to go. It's the man behind the wheel that's to blame.
- Some of the biggest rooms in hell will be crowded full of church members.
- Don't take away from teachers the right to punish kids. I wore four pairs of pants when I went to school.

During his career Sunday preached twenty thousand times! In 1917 in New York, a million and a half people heard him during a ten-week crusade. Over one million people, it is said, gave their hearts to God during his campaigns, which spanned a quarter of a century.

Photo courtesy of Winona Lake Bible Conference

Sunday School

Chained to their benches, learning to read and write . . .

Does this sound like a class of Sunday school pupils to you?

The year was 1780, and newspaper publisher Robert Raikes was concerned about the delinquency problem among poor young people in Gloucester, England. So he put together a list of ninety pupil prospects and hired a lady to teach them "readin', writin', 'rithmetic, and religion" on Sundays, the only day the children had off from factory work. In those days, no public schools existed, and only the rich could afford education. When word spread of the opportunities Sunday school education could bring, no one needed to chain pupils down to keep them in. In the first fifty years,

Sunday schools grew to attract more than 1.3 million pupils in Britain and the United States.

In America, the founding of public schools made Sunday schools into places that taught religion only. The Sunday school moved west in the 1800s with the help of Sunday school missionaries, who rode from town to town organizing their schools and selling books. The most famous missionary, Stephen Paxton, once set up forty-seven Sunday schools in forty days. His horse's name was Robert Raikes!

Once a town set up its own Sunday school, it usually could then establish its own church and public school.

In the city of Toronto, Canada, stands a statue of Robert Raikes—a tribute to his vision and the vast Sunday school movement. In 1980 the Sunday school celebrated its 200th anniversary.

Sunday School Attendance

Trying for a good Sunday school attendance record? Here's a target to shoot for. As of this writing, Roland E. Daab of Columbia, Illinois, has attended classes for 3,351 consecutive Sundays—an unbroken period of more than sixty-four years!

Super Gang

What in the world is Super Gang? Well, it's a traveling troupe of talented kids from St. Louis who are telling other kids that it's fun to be a Christian. Super Gang has appeared on tv, recorded two albums, and toured all around the United States.

Super Gang was started by Tom Brooks and his wife Robin. The pair combined his background in Las Vegas show business (before his conversion) with her talents in Christian education to come up with a new way to help kids know about Christ. The resulting show follows a gang of Christian kids and their zany friends through tough,

real-life situations. Those acting in the Super Gang show range in age from six to fourteen, and were chosen by audition from among Christian kids in the St. Louis area.

The Super Gang made its tv debut on a Christmas special for St. Louis's KMOX-TV, a CBS affiliate. Later they made another tv special for the 700 Club. In July 1982 they sang at the World's Fair in Knoxville.

"The crowds went wild as the gang was singing and dancing," reported *Super News*, the official newsletter of Super Gang, about the Knoxville show. "The Lord really blessed the performances and many children and adults heard about Jesus for the first time."

"We show kids how Jesus can work in their day-to-day lives, in school where their friends are, where their friends don't know the Lord, and at home with Mom and Dad," Tom Brooks explains.

Already Super Gang clubs are springing up in the United States, Great Britain, Canada, Australia, and New Zealand.

FREE: Super Action Pack

Any born-again Christian can join Super Gang, just by sending his testimony in to Super Gang headquarters. All Super Gang members receive an action pack loaded with "Super Stuff."

This includes your official Super Gang badge, your own personal Super Gang member card—signed by "Preacher Pigeon," super stickers, super tracts to give to your friends, a letter from Son Shine, plus your first copy of the *Super News*, the Gang's newsletter.

And it's all free. It's Super Gang's way of welcoming you into God's family.

Write Super Gang Headquarters, P.O. Box 2128, Maryland Heights, Missouri 63043.

Surgeon General

Some would call him the nation's number one friend of children. His name is Dr. C. Everett Koop. His position: the nation's surgeon general.

You may think of the surgeon general only as the man who puts out all those warnings that cigarette smoking "may be hazardous to your health." That's true, but that's not his main job. He heads up the seven thousand employees of the United States Public Health Service, and is spokesman for the president in telling the nation's health care goals. His appointment has to be approved by Congress.

Dr. Koop has always specialized in treating children. As the chief surgeon of Philadelphia's Children's Hospital, he saved the lives of thousands of children.

A few years ago, he successfully separated Siamese twins born of a mother from Puerto Rico, and his fame spread around the world. He refused to charge the family for this operation because they were poor.

Dr. Koop believes the Bible has some strong words to say to America today about saving the lives of children. This includes deformed children and even unborn children still in the mother's womb. He coauthored a book on this subject with Francis Schaeffer, called *Whatever Happened to the Human Race?* and appeared in a Christian film by the same name.

Some have strongly criticized Koop for his "pro-life" views, and even tried to block his appointment as Surgeon General.

But *Life* magazine profiled him with admiration as "a man of strong convictions."

"When you've got absolutes that you feel are God-given," *Life* quoted Koop as saying, "you don't have much room for compromise on right or wrong."

Dr. Koop was formerly Surgeon in Chief at Philadelphia's Children's Hospital.

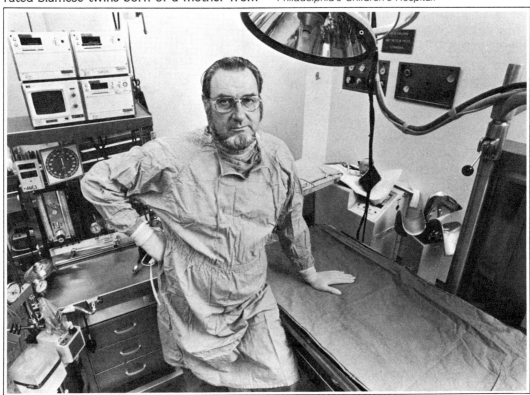

Photo courtesy of Philadelphia Children's Hospital

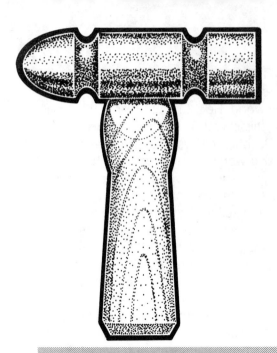

Talent Plus

Carrie Meier of St. Louis is just twelve years old, but you wouldn't believe all the things this talented kid has been up to.

She has done television commercials in the St. Louis area for more than a dozen firms, including McDonald's, Dairy Queen, and Pizza Hut.

She has appeared on "I Love You, St. Louis" billboards, and pushed Toyota cars for the Japanese market.

She was one of five finalists (out of more than five hundred) in the screen test for the title role in the movie *Annie*.

She has appeared in all kinds of stage plays, concerts, fashion shows, and variety shows. She has also appeared on tv's "Incredible Kids," and on "The PTL Club."

Carrie's talents in "show biz" first began to show up when she was five. At that age she begged her parents to send her to piano lessons. Carrie's piano teacher recognized the girl's "sparkle" and suggested she do commercials. So, beginning at age five, Carrie did!

Carrie became a Christian back when she was eight years old. "While I was attending Bible camp, I suddenly realized that I was missing something very big—having Christ in my heart," she remembers.

Now, besides her many other activities, Carrie tours with the St. Louis-based Christian troupe, Super Gang (see *Super Gang*).

Teen Missions

Down in Florida, at Merritt Island, there's a most unusual "boot camp." Here each year, in a junglelike setting, nearly two thousand teenagers from across the United States endure a rugged two weeks that would match the best of jungle training camps.

They pick their way through obstacle courses, climb rope ladders, bathe from a pan, and sleep in tents tucked way back in the woods.

They also learn to mix mortar, lay blocks, tie steel, cook without stoves—and even sing in foreign languages.

That's because these teens know they'll soon head abroad, in scores of summer task forces, to complete work projects and share Christ in countries around the world.

It's all a part of the program of Teen Missions International, founded in 1970 by Bob Bland. Mr. Bland had seen the potential of Christian teens to make a real impact in the world. And so he set out to harness their energy.

In one recent summer alone, these teens could be found in twenty-four different countries.

- In Israel they built a home for boys.
- In Alaska they helped construct a Bible camp.
- In Honduras they built a radio tower and refabricked an airplane.
- In Australia they built a house for missionaries.
- In the Dominican Republic they rebuilt a church destroyed by a hurricane.
- In Germany they converted an old farm into a youth camp.
- In Papua New Guinea, they built a jungle airstrip on the top of a remote mountain. And the list goes on.

These kids have become known far and wide as ones who aren't afraid to use their muscles to help God's work around the world. They have laid untold thousands of bricks and concrete blocks. And for that privilege, they also have to raise their own financial support!

Many of these kids have also spread the gospel of Jesus Christ. In the United States and abroad they have established teen hot lines (see *Dial-a-Teen*), held street meetings, visited nursing homes, and worked in Vacation Bible Schools.

Of course, neither the boot camp, nor the overseas experience, is all work. It's also a time of great joy and fun. Says Kim Roof, who helped construct buildings in Australia, "We even had to make our own bricks from the clay on the property. But we also did some sight-seeing. We were able to see kangaroos, koala bears, platypuses, and other animals unique to Australia. The Lord opened churches to us, and more importantly he opened the hearts of people to himself."

You have to be at least thirteen years of age to join a Teen Missions project. If you want to know more, simply write: Teen Missions International, P.O. Box 1056, Merritt Island, Florida 32952.

Jungle training includes a difficult obstacle course.

Photo courtesy of Teen Missions International

Teen Television Station

Teenagers run a television station? That's right. The $2.5 million YFC-TV (Channel 50), which is owned and operated by Kansas City's Youth for Christ, signed on the air on December of 1979.

To a large extent, teenagers handle the station's cameras, programming, and engineering load.

It is no second-rate operation either. With the best of equipment, the staff has been turning out quality talk shows, musicals, dramas, and other programming, some of it for national syndication.

If you visit the Kansas City area, you can tour the studios during the day. And if you're in town on a Saturday night, you can join nearly two thousand other teenagers in the nation's largest weekly Christian youth rally, held on Youth for Christ properties at 4715 Rainbow Boulevard in the suburb of Shawnee Mission.

Television Studios

The Christian Broadcasting Network (CBN) in Virginia Beach, Virginia, has "the finest equipment available in American TV," according to the *Saturday Evening Post*.

Studio seven, home of "The 700 Club," is one-fourth the size of a football field. It has a remote-control, push-button, computer-based staging system that allows fifty-three pieces of scenery to be moved at one time—without human stagehands!

Actors work on the set of "Another Life."

Photo courtesy of CBN

193

Tony the Tiger

You've seen Tony the Tiger on breakfast cereal boxes, and you've heard his growl on tv. He's a friendly tiger, of course. And he loves his Kellogg's Sugar Frosted Flakes.

The voice of Tony the Tiger is really Thurl Ravenscroft, who used to sing bass for The Old-Fashioned Revival Hour Quartet, famous in gospel music.

Your parents may remember the quartet. Ask them. If they don't believe Mr. Ravenscroft is the real Tony, tell them it's the "gospel" truth.

Touching the Sky

Where is the world's tallest church spire? In downtown Chicago, at the First Methodist Church on Clark Street. The building consists of a 22-story skyscraper, with a parsonage at the 330-foot level. A "Sky Chapel" sits at the 400-foot level. The steeple cross which tops it all off is 568 feet above the street.

Treehouse Club

Almost every kid likes to climb into a treehouse. Ken Anderson, who has produced a lot of exciting films for kids (see *Films*), has a couple of remarkable treehouses in the backwoods section of his farm near Warsaw, Indiana. One has three stories!

Even if you don't have a good treehouse in your backyard or nearby, you can still join the Treehouse Club. This is a television program produced by Child Evangelism Fellowship, and aired on more than two hundred tv stations since 1970. Young viewers are drawn into the program with puppets, skits, activity scenes, and music—and they will always hear the gospel.

For more information about joining the Treehouse Club, consult your local television guide, or write: Child Evangelism Fellowship, Warrenton, Missouri 63383.

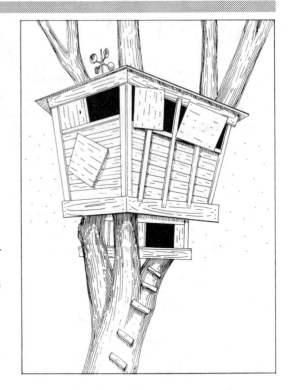

Truckers for Jesus

In downtown Louisville, Kentucky, an amazed storekeeper told one of his customers, "Would you believe there are several hundred truckers over at the hotel, and they're carrying Bibles and talking about Jesus stuff!"

It was the annual convention of Transport for Christ, truckers who, as they crisscross the country with their heavy loads, try to lighten the personal loads of others by sharing the good news of Jesus.

The Christian truckers' movement has its chaplains—all former truck drivers themselves—who know and understand the trucker's life. One large Sapp Brothers truck plaza in Omaha, advertised as "the world's largest coffeepot," even has its own chaplain on duty twenty-four hours a day. Truckers stop there for services.

Truck chaplains show safety films at truck terminals, hold religious services, and meet other needs. You may see one of their mobile chapels on the highway, a sleek eighteen wheeler with a small cross above its air horns.

And many of the CB calls on the road will probably be directed to another "good buddy" in Jesus.

Tunnel Vision

In Jerusalem each year, blind high school students tour an historic, ancient tunnel that runs for one-third of a mile beneath the city. The tunnel was built twenty-seven hundred years ago by King Hezekiah of Judah, to give Jerusalem water during the siege of Sennacherib. (This attack is described in the Bible in II Kings 19—20.)

But how can blind students, you may wonder, "see" the tunnel they're passing through, or even find their way?

Believe it or not, before the students leave the classroom, they know exactly where they're going.

That's because James Fleming, Jerusalem correspondent for the magazine *Biblical Archaeology Review*, knows how to make fantastic relief maps from clay. He has

made one of Jerusalem so that blind students can feel the contours of the city and "let their fingers do the walking" across town.

Fleming has also built a clay model of Hezekiah's tunnel and its twenty-five niches of special interest. This includes the places where the ancient tunnelers made mistakes and tunneled in the wrong direction, then corrected themselves. The students can also feel the place where the two ends of the tunnel meet (King Hezekiah had it dug from both ends simultaneously). By the time they make the trip, they have memorized all twenty-five points and know all about the biblical and archaeological background of the site.

Blind students themselves, in fact, are positioned at these special interest points along the way, to brief the others about what they're "seeing."

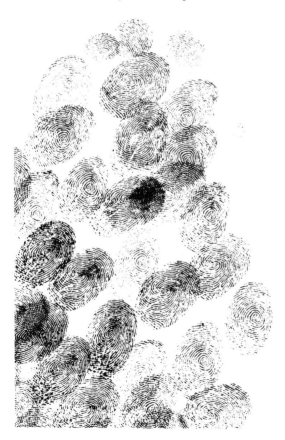

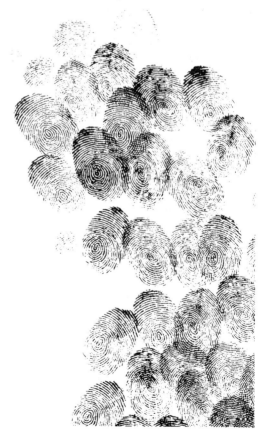

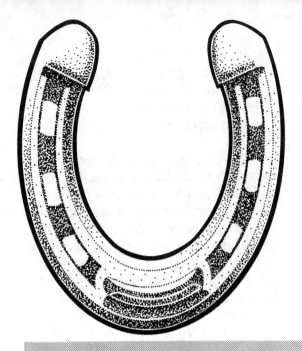

Uncle Cam

"He'll never last two months," said a veteran missionary when he saw the skinny, twenty-one-year-old Cameron Townsend get off the steamship in Guatemala in 1917.

But he had underestimated the energy and determination of young Townsend, who had come to Central America to sell Spanish Bibles—and would later found the world-renowned mission of Wycliffe Bible Translators.

Cam Townsend tramped the back trails of Guatemala, Honduras, El Salvador, and Nicaragua on foot or on muleback with his Bibles. "Sometimes the jungle would grow so ominously dense," describes a *Reader's Digest* article, "that he would hike with his hat bobbing on a long stick held out before him—to fool the jaguars."

Cam survived the swarms of jungle insects, and learned to eat such treats as bugs, worms, and fried tadpoles. But his work troubled him. What good were Spanish Bibles when so many of the Indians neither spoke nor read Spanish?

One day along his way, Townsend plopped down to rest beside an old Cakchi-quel Indian, pulled a Bible from his backpack, and gave the man a cheery "Buenas tardes." The Indian returned only a grunt. Townsend babbled on in Spanish in an attempt to share the gospel. Finally the Indian blurted out in his own Cakchiquel tongue, "If your God is so great, why can't he speak my language?"

Townsend knew only a few Cakchiquel words, but it was enough for him to pick up the Indian's point.

That's when it all began. Townsend set out to learn the Cakchiquel language, even

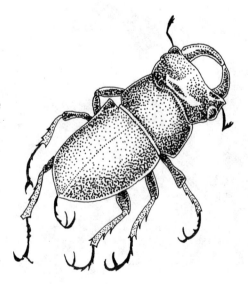

though he had no linguistic training. He was the first outsider who had ever attempted it. He built a house of logs and cornstalks among the Indians and settled in to stay. After twelve hardworking years, he had learned the complex language, reduced it to writing (it had never before been written), and produced a Cakchiquel New Testament, which he then presented to the president of Guatemala. In the meantime he had also built schools, a clinic, a printing press, and an orphanage. Soon the power of the New Testament in their own tongue began to transform the Indian tribe. Churches sprang up. Witchcraft decreased.

Townsend knew that possibly a thousand tribes in Latin America alone had no written language. He had to have help. So he recruited a handful of students and trained them to do what he had done. That's how it began. Today Wycliffe has more than four thousand missionaries.

In the earlier days it would take a missionary up to a month, often paddling down crocodile-infested rivers, to reach a tribe. Supplies had to be shuttled in the same way. Cam said that was far too slow. So he called for Christian pilots and launched a "missionary air force" called JAARS (Jungle Aviation And Radio Service).

He soon took the work of Wycliffe onto other continents—to India, the Philippines, Papua New Guinea, Vietnam, and Indonesia, and then on to Africa.

Even Soviet Russia, he believed, would eventually let him in. "Incredible!" said his critics. "No way!" They were wrong. The prestigious Soviet Academy of Sciences, though officially atheistic, permitted Wycliffe to translate a section of the New Testament into several Soviet tribal languages!

During his lifetime, while opening doors for Wycliffe in country after country, Townsend slept in jungle hammocks and government palaces. He was equally at home with peasant and president. One goal consumed "Uncle Cam," as people affectionately called him: to make it possible for every person alive to read the Bible.

Wycliffe is now at work in more than a thousand tribes of the world, but there are still three thousand languages to go. The work is accelerating. "Uncle Cam" Townsend didn't see it finished in his lifetime, but maybe you will.

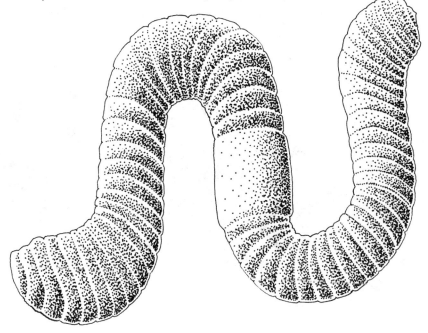

Underground Railroad

An old building in Fountain City, Indiana, near the Ohio border, may have been the busiest hiding place in the nation in the early 1800s. This privately owned home has often been called the "Grand Central Station" of the Underground Railroad. It belonged to Levi and Catharine Coffin, Quakers who opposed the South's slavery system so strongly that they opened their home to fugitive slaves who needed help on their flight to freedom into Canada.

Over a period of twenty years, some two thousand fugitives passed through their hands. Not one of them was ever captured!

On occasion the garret was used as a place of concealment, and even the space between strawtick and feather bed (two layers of homemade mattress). Rough cots in the attic provided extra sleeping space.

One of the refugees who stayed there was Eliza, whose story is told in *Uncle Tom's Cabin*, by Harriet Beecher Stowe. The Coffins were the models for Simeon and Rachel Halliday of that classic.

Why did the Coffins do all this? They may well have felt it a mandate from God to help black people, who were also his children. Isaiah 1:17 could have been their motto: "Seek judgment, relieve the oppressed."

United States Capitol

The Capitol building, the seat of United States government where Congress meets, looms at the end of Washington, D.C.'s Pennsylvania Avenue. It's on a little rise of land, so that's why you may hear the term "Capitol Hill." Some other facts you should know:

• George Washington laid the cornerstone in 1793.

• The British burned the Capitol in 1814. President James Madison and his wife had to flee the city into Virginia along back roads. If you visit the Capitol, you can still climb the same spiral stairway that the invading British used.

• If you want to watch the proceedings of Congress while it is in session, someone will have to get you a pass from your local congressman.

• In each house, as you face the Speaker's dais, Republicans will be on your right, Democrats on your left.

• Each house has its own chaplain, and sessions each day open in prayer. This tradition began two years before the Declaration of Independence.

• Just off the rotunda of the Capitol is a room set aside for the private prayer and meditation of members of Congress. It is not open to the public. The room's focal point is a stained glass-window showing George Washington kneeling in prayer.

• From the Capitol you can ride one of the electric cars in a unique subway system that runs from the Capitol to the Senate and House office buildings.

SEND FOR: Replica of Capitol

Here is a miniature replica of the United States Capitol that you can put together. You will find in the kit the pieces for the building and base, printed in color on paper card stock. You cut them out and glue them together. Includes a booklet on the Capitol's history. Send $2.50 plus $1 postage and handling to: Kenilworth Press, Box 469, Cortland, New York 13045.

Make these cardboard pages into the Capitol.

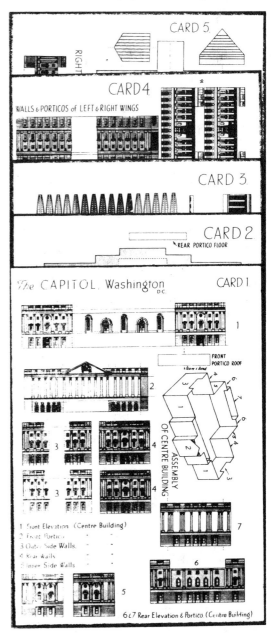

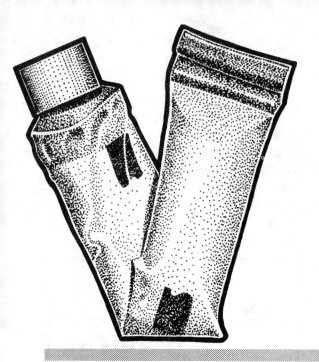

Volcanoes

On May 18, 1980, the interior of Mount St. Helens in the Washington Cascades was rumbling and leaking steam. Suddenly, at 8:32 A.M., the mountain blew.

The great blast took more than a thousand feet off the top of the mountain and devastated the forest for miles. Volcanic ash shot more than sixty thousand feet into the air and then began to drift eastward across the United States.

Before Mount St. Helens's eruption, most Americans probably assumed volcanoes only happened in other parts of the world. Most knew about the great explosion of Mount Vesuvius in Italy in A.D. 79, which buried the city of Pompeii. Or perhaps they'd heard of Hawaii's Mauna Loa, the world's tallest volcano, which rises thirty thousand feet from the floor of the Pacific Ocean.

Mount St. Helens, however, is not the Northwest's only volcanic peak. So also are Mount Rainier near Seattle, Mount Hood near Portland, and northern California's Mount Shasta. Oregon's Crater Lake once was also a volcano. It "blew its top" more than five thousand years ago. Snow and rainwater filled in the crater to create the

beautiful scene that exists there today.

In fact, scientists tell us that a huge layer of volcanic basalt underlies much of Washington, Oregon, Idaho, and Nevada—down even into northern California. Imagine the explosion it would have taken to create this huge lava flow!

So many great volcanoes surround the Pacific Ocean, in fact, that people have called it the "Ring of Fire."

There are also many volcanoes under the sea, called "seamounts," or, if they are flat-topped, "guyots."

Some scientists who also believe the Bible theorize that these underwater volcanoes may have formed during Noah's flood. Mount Ararat in Turkey, mentioned in the Bible's flood story, is a volcanic mountain.

The evidence suggests that volcanic activity was much greater during the earlier history of the earth. If so, we can be thankful that it has subsided.

For volcanoes can be tremendously destructive. Indonesia's Mount Tambora erupted in 1815 with six million times the energy of an atomic bomb, and killed 12,000 people. Krakatoa's explosion in 1883 caused tidal waves that killed 36,000 on neighboring Pacific islands. Worst of all, the lava and hot gas from the eruption of

Photo courtesy of the National Park Service

Mauna Loa is the world's tallest volcano.

Mount Pelée in the French West Indies in 1902 wiped out the town of Saint-Pierre. The sole survivor from among some 38,000 townsfolk was a man deep in the town dungeon.

An eruption like that of Mount St. Helens does point us again to the terrifying power of our Creator.

FREE: Volcanic Ash

You may live a long way from remote St. Helens, but you can have a sample of its volcanic ash right on the shelf in your bedroom. Discover firsthand what it looks and feels like. Your one-ounce vial will come with a note that explains what volcanic ash is. Write to: Dean Foster Nurseries, Route 2, Hartford, Michigan 49057. Enclose fifty cents for postage and handling.

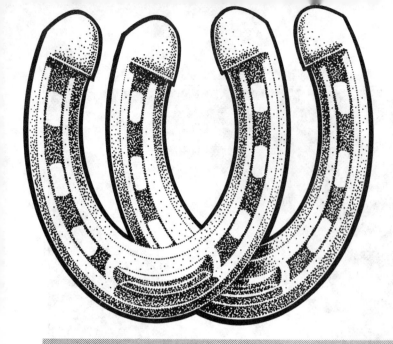

Walk Across America

On one of North Carolina's Appalachian mountainsides, redheaded Peter Jenkins, weary from a heavy backpack and a forty-mile hike, eased himself down against the trunk of a tree.

His one-hundred-pound Alaskan malamute, Cooper, stretched out alongside him.

Jenkins had set out on foot from his home in south central New York state to discover "the real America." In his college years, it seemed the nation had been falling apart: racial violence, political scandal, student protest.

America—should he love it or leave it? Jenkins decided he would *walk* from coast to coast, mingle and live among the people, and give America one last chance.

After intensive physical training, he began. And once on the trail, Jenkins saw hope. In his story for *National Geographic* Magazine, later packaged into a best-selling book, *A Walk Across America,* he says to the operator of a little country store, "I've come to realize what a bad press America's been giving itself. There's a lot of good in it that also needs telling. The land, the geography—they're unbelievable. And the people! I haven't gone a day that someone I met hasn't been kind, or thoughtful, or helpful. Plain, simple, ordinary folks they may be, but they're heroes to me."

Peter Jenkins began to realize that his trek was a quest not only to find the real America, but also to find the meaning of his own life.

One night in Mobile, Alabama, while on his way to what a friend had said would be a "real wild party," Jenkins saw a sign for

Peter and Cooper walked America together.

a Christian evangelistic crusade. He decided to go there instead.

"Ten thousand people packed the auditorium," describes Jenkins in *National Geographic*. "I sat down front so I could take some pictures, feeling just a bit silly at being there.

"Then up to the podium strode the evangelist, a tall, tough Texan who looked more like a linebacker for the Dallas Cowboys than a preacher. But a preacher he was."

At the close of the meeting, Jenkins and about three hundred others walked to the podium at the evangelist's invitation:

Do you accept Jesus as your personal Savior? he asked us.

My lips opened. I said I did. I meant it.

Again he asked, again each of us replied, affirming our acceptance.

Later, relaxed and clear-eyed and more inwardly at peace than I had ever been, I floated out of there and back into the street.

I never did get to that real wild party.

"A Walk Across America" became the most popular article *National Geographic* has ever published. Partway through his walk, Jenkins married a Christian girl in New Orleans. The two eventually continued the cross-country trek, reaching the Pacific Ocean on the Oregon coastline in January 1979. Peter had walked some three thousand miles! *National Geographic* carried a final installment, and a book sequel, *The Walk West*, has become another best-seller.

Walls of Jerusalem?

Startled travelers do a double take these days when they suddenly look up to see the walls of Jerusalem—in the middle of Arkansas!

Around the main gate, which is exactly like the one you can still see today in far-off Old Jerusalem, several camels often linger. One may even have a rider, dressed as if he had just stepped out of the Bible.

How did this come about? Some years ago a man who wanted Americans to know what the land of the Bible is really like, decided to build a replica of the Old City of Jerusalem in the Ozarks. It is not a model. He decided to build it life-size!

The section of the giant five-story wall and the Golden Gate that is already com-pleted will be the entrance to this replica city. Completing the project will cost millions of dollars.

Some say the replica city is such a huge undertaking that it will never be finished. But who really knows?

Wandering Wheels

Have you ever gone on a bike hike? Unless you go bicycling a lot, the twenty or thirty miles you travel will probably make your legs feel like jelly when you're done! Yet it's a fun way to travel and get a close-up look at the scenery around you.

The teens and young adults that sign up for the Wandering Wheels program make a whole summer out of bike hikes. Traveling in groups of six, they bicycle all the way across the United States, averaging one hundred miles a day!

It's a rugged program of self-discipline and physical endurance. The cyclists have crossed mountain passes higher than eleven thousand feet, and pedaled into desert temperatures as high as 120 degrees.

Part of the trip's purpose is to provide time for thought, away from life's distractions. The cyclists learn quickly what it's like to let go of the luxuries. There's no air conditioning, and no color television. They learn to cope with stress.

Another purpose of the trip is witness. The Wheel kids rub shoulders with townsfolk on the way, and sleep in gymnasiums and church basements or out in the open.

Sometimes they receive the keys of the city. The cyclists have sung to two presidents: Harry Truman and Lyndon Johnson.

Though not a choir, they sing together a lot. They sing the songs of the faith, and talk to others about Jesus Christ.

A final purpose is learning teamwork. One group escorted a blind boy across the United States on a tandem bicycle. Another participated with a young man with only one leg.

You have to be at least fifteen years old to qualify for Wandering Wheels. If you're interested, write for information to:

Wandering Wheels, Taylor University, Up-land, Indiana 46989.

FREE: Bicycle Patch

Huffy Corporation has an official bike patch that it will send you free. It shows red and orange bicyclists against a field of navy blue. For your bike jeans patch, write: Advertising, Huffy Corporation, P.O. Box 1204, Dayton, Ohio 45401. Include fifty cents for postage and handling.

FREE: Bike Tour Information

The Backroads Bicycle Touring Company specializes in week or weekend tours through places like the Colorado Rockies, Yellowstone, Big Sur, and other scenic spots. But you have to be at least ten years old, and accompanied by a parent or guardian.

If you want to learn more, send a business-sized, self-addressed, stamped envelope to: Backroads Bicycle Touring Company, P.O. Box 5534, Berkeley, California 94705.

Wardrobe

If you're a fan of C. S. Lewis's book *The Lion, the Witch, and the Wardrobe,* you'll be interested to learn that there *is* a real wardrobe.

That is, there is a real piece of furniture called a wardrobe, from the house in Belfast, Ireland, where C. S. Lewis grew up. Lewis's grandfather handcarved the piece, and Lewis and his brother Warren played in it as children. You can see the wardrobe in its new home in the Marion E. Wade Collection at the library of Wheaton College, an hour west of Chicago, Illinois.

But don't be hopeful about finding anything unusual when you look inside the wardrobe. "The first thing kids want to do is open the door and see if there's a back," said one librarian, referring to the fact that the back of the wardrobe opened into the land of Narnia in Lewis's classic.

There may be nothing magical to see in the Wade Collection, but there are plenty of items of interest to Lewis fans, including copies of many letters he wrote to children, plus a group of stories he authored between the ages of ten and fourteen with his brother Warren's help. The stories, dubbed "The Boxen Manuscripts," are about a world of toy animals, and the Lewis brothers illustrated their work themselves.

The Wade Collection is primarily a study center. Before visiting, call (312) 260-5908, as viewing hours are limited, or write to: Wade Collection, Wheaton College, Wheaton, Illinois 60187.

Webster, Noah

When you want to know how to spell a word for that school report, you probably try to find a dictionary. Many such dictionaries carry the name of Webster. Does yours?

The brilliant Noah Webster, author of the finest English dictionary of his time, could do almost anything. He practiced law, launched a daily newspaper in New York, and helped establish a college. He also moved among famous friends. Noah Webster routinely rubbed shoulders with men like George Washington, Ben Franklin, Alexander Hamilton, and John Jay.

Like a human computer, Webster systematized in his mind and in his huge files of clippings almost every piece of knowledge he acquired. When he was in his twenties, he put together an elementary school spelling book and grammar book.

But at the age of forty, Noah Webster began to feel that perhaps he was resting his religious faith more on his own accomplishments than on the simple grace of God. That's when this great man started to study the Bible on his own, as never before. One evening he cast himself down before God, confessed his sins, and asked for pardon for Jesus' sake.

The next morning he called his family together and, with deep emotion, told them that for years he had neglected one of his most important duties as father—family prayer.

It took Noah Webster more than thirty years of his life to complete his *American Dictionary*, but during those years he also found time to continue his study of the Bible. Certain definitions in those earlier editions reflect his Christian stance.

The day Noah Webster finally finished the dictionary, he and his wife knelt to thank God for the great occasion.

Noah Webster's dictionary had seventy thousand entries, and was the most complete English dictionary done at that time. His name still appears on the dictionary today that lists the most English words: *Webster's Third New International Dictionary*. Published by G. & C. Merriam Company, this dictionary has 450,000 entries!

WheatWonders

The Midwest each year produces the largest grain crop in the world. But many people do not realize that Christians played two major roles in this success story.

Devout Mennonite immigrants from Russia came to central Kansas in 1874. They brought with them a hardy winter grain seed, now famous as Turkey Red. It turned out to be ideally suited to crop-growing conditions in the Midwest, and in time it helped to establish Kansas as the Wheat State and the "Breadbasket of the Nation."

The "Wheat Palace" at Goessel, Kansas, stands as a tribute to those early Christian immigrants. The palace contains a replica of the Liberty Bell—made of wheat!

The other Christian contributor to grain agriculture was an inventor. Farmers used to have to harvest wheat by hand. Then in 1831, Cyrus H. McCormick invented the world's first mechanical harvesting machine. It transformed agriculture not only in the United States, but around the globe. Many Mennonite farmers were able to use it.

You may have heard that McCormick was an inventor and great industrialist. But did you know that he was also an outspoken Christian? He gave his money generously to help spread the gospel. His son, Cyrus H. McCormick, Jr., served for six years as one of the original trustees of Chicago's Moody Bible Institute.

You can read more about the life of the Mennonite families on the Kansas frontier in *Turkey Red* and its sequel, *Harvest Gold* by Esther Loewen Vogt (from David C. Cook Publishing Co.).

Wilson, Woodrow

Do you ever get restless in church?

A boy who would someday become president used to spend many hours in the pews of a Presbyterian church in Augusta, Georgia. Usually he listened patiently to the sermons, but sometimes he, too, got restless.

It's not unusual, of course, to find presidents who once sat in church. But in the case of little Woodrow Wilson, he had special reason to pay attention.

His father was the minister!

Witherspoon, John

There are stong feelings today about whether or not preachers should be involved in politics.

John Witherspoon, highly respected Presbyterian clergyman and president of what is now Princeton, didn't think ministers should preach politics from the pulpit.

But as an *individual* Christian citizen, Witherspoon, a keen political observer, let himself be elected a delegate to the historic Continental Congress.

On July 4, 1776, he stood in a burst of eloquence and said that to hesitate to declare independence would be "to consent to our own slavery." Witherspoon shouted that he would rather die by the hand of the executioner "than desert at this crisis the sacred cause of my country."

When he finished, there was dead silence.

John Hancock ordered a reading of the final draft, then called for the vote, colony by colony. When it was over, the decision was unanimous. The secretary placed the document on the speaker's table and looked at the president of the congress.

He fingered his goose-quill pen. Then with a flourish and bold strokes, John Hancock put his signature on one of history's most daring documents.

John Witherspoon, the only clergyman to sign the Declaration of Independence, had been in the right place at the right time.

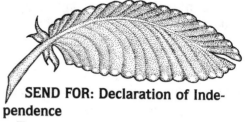

SEND FOR: Declaration of Independence

To obtain an authentic replica of this important document of 1776, complete with signatures, see instructions under *Columbus*.

World Land Record Holder

On December 17, 1979, in California's Mojave Desert, Stan Barrett streaked down the space shuttle runway at Edwards Air Force Base in a sixty thousand horsepower rocket car. That day he became the first man ever to break the sound barrier on land. His speed: an astounding 739 miles per hour!

Earlier Barrett had made nine runs on the Bonneville Salt Flats in Utah in that same rocket car, and had set a new world land speed record at 638 mph. But the surface of the salt flats, Barrett found, was not suitable for high enough speeds to

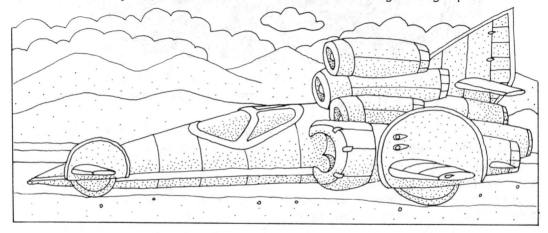

break the sound barrier. That's why he changed to the Mojave Desert. Interestingly, it was in the skies over this same desert in 1949 that test pilot Chuck Yeager broke the sound barrier for the first time, launching man into the era of supersonic flight.

Even at the Mojave Desert, it took Barrett nine runs to break the sound barrier on land. And that was only with assistance of a sidewinder missile, which added an extra twelve thousand horsepower to his forty-eight thousand horsepower hybrid rocket motor!

"There was just one slight problem with the sidewinder," says Barrett. "Once you turned it on, you couldn't turn it off. And I had to turn it on at 610 miles per hour."

It took a lot of faith in the car and the scientists who had designed it, says Barrett, to push the button and light the missile.

But the sound barrier was not the biggest barrier he's broken, Barrett notes.

"The most important decision I ever made was when I accepted Jesus Christ into my life, thus breaking the barrier that exists between myself and God," he says.

Writing

Do you enjoy writing? Or has something happened to you that you'd like to share? If so, you could submit a story or article to a Christian youth magazine.

The following magazines may be interested in your work. But *The Christian Kids Almanac* advises that you "query" them first. That means tell them briefly what your story or idea is, and see if they are interested. Or, ask them what kind of material they might be looking for from someone your age.

We recommend you try:

● *Counselor.* A Sunday school paper for kids from third through sixth grade. Write to them at Box 513, Glen Ellyn, Illinois 60137.

● *Sprint.* A Sunday school paper for junior highers. Write in care of David C. Cook Publishing Company, 850 N. Grove Avenue, Elgin, Illinois 60120.

● *Teen Power.* A Sunday school paper for younger teens. Write to them at Box 513, Glen Ellyn, Illinois 60137.

● *Telling the Truth.* A magazine for teens. They may even invite you to be a campus correspondent! Write them at 12814 U.S. 41 North, Evansville, Indiana 47711.

● *Trails.* For elementary school boys and girls. Write them at Box 788, Wheaton, Illinois 60187.

● *Young Ambassador.* A magazine for young teens. Your best chance might be YA's annual contest, with categories including fiction, first-person experience, and devotional writing. Write for information to Box 82808, Lincoln, Nebraska 68501.

Your local church paper or denominational publication may also be able to use your talent. (If you have a poetic bent, look up *Poetry.*)

Xmas

We recognize the letters *Xmas* as an abbreviation for "Christmas." Some Christians have interpreted this shortened form to mean that Christ has been left out of Christmas, and this may be true in many cases.

But dictionaries tell us that the *X* is actually an ancient abbreviation for *Christ.* It is the symbol for the Greek *X*, or *chi*, the first letter of *Christos.* Even the abbreviated *Xmas* can point to Jesus!

So that no one misunderstands what the holiday is about, however, it might still be best to spell out the word *Christmas* when you use it.

All of these ancient Christian symbols incorporate X, the Greek letter called chi, *which was the first letter of the Greek word for Christ. Many also include P, or* ro, *the second letter of the Greek word for Christ.*

This symbol combines I, the first letter of Jesus' name in Greek, with the X.

This is a decorative version of the chi-ro monogram.

Here the chi-ro *is combined with* I, H, *and* S, *the first, second, and last letters of Jesus' name.*

The chi-ro *here blends with* alpha *and* omega, *first and last letters of the alphabet (see Revelation 1:8).*

This chi-ro *is surrounded by the Greek letters that spell fish. The fish was a common Christian symbol because the five letters stand for the words* Jesus Christ God's Son Savior *in Greek.*

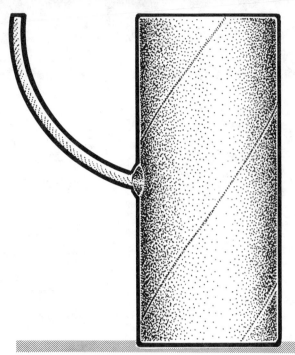

Young Life

Young Life clubs in suburban America reach out to seventy-five thousand teenagers—in junior high and in high school—each week. And through the summer, teenagers swarm into several Young Life resort properties, from British Columbia to Colorado to North Carolina.

The weekly club program—designed for fun for Christians and non-Christians both—includes the singing of contemporary songs, plus a Christian message. The club director will also hold a weekly Bible study for those more interested in the Christian faith.

The Young Life ranches combine outdoor

fun (in spectacular settings!) with spiritual growth and fellowship with other teens from across the country. Young Life also has a lodge in Colorado where parents can stay, not far from the Frontier Ranch for teens.

For information on the Young Life club programs or Young Life ranches, write to: Young Life, Box 520, Colorado Springs, Colorado 80901.

Youth for Christ

Youth for Christ (YFC) is a Christian movement specializing in outreach to teenagers. Today it is best known for its twelve hundred Campus Life clubs across the United States. The clubs' weekly meetings—designed for bringing your friends to—include zany games and a Christian message. The club leader will also conduct a weekly Bible study for those wanting a deeper look at spiritual truths.

YFC also sponsors camps, rallies, and conferences, and is affiliated with the magazine *Campus Life* (see *Magazines*). Among those on the YFC board is singer Johnny Cash.

Youth for Christ also has a media ministry of television and radio programs. The initial "Johnny Cash Youth Special" was on tv across the country between June 1978 and January 1981. The program combined drama, testimonies, entertainment, and interviews to present the needs of youth today and the way Youth for Christ's staff and programs help to meet those needs.

YFC's second prime-time tv special, entitled "Is There a Family in the House?" began airing in March 1981.

For more information on Campus Life clubs or other programs, write: Youth for Christ, 360 South Main Place, Wheaton, Illinois 60187.

Youth with a Mission

Young people can be used, even on a short-term basis, to reach the world for Jesus Christ. That's why in 1960 Loren Cunningham founded Youth with a Mission (YWAM). *Time* magazine reports that ten thousand people are involved each year in YWAM's short-term projects around the world.

Ministering in some two hundred countries, YWAM specializes in creative ways to reach others with the gospel: from drama troupes to work in nutrition and agriculture! The mission makes a special effort to have Christian young people witnessing at such international events as the Olympics, World Cup Soccer games, and Expos. They even own a large ship, the *Anastasis*, which sails the oceans to evangelize in the ports of the world (see *Ocean Travelers*).

Those who join YWAM must be at least eighteen and must raise their own financial support. For more information write: Youth with a Mission, Box 4600, Tyler, Texas 75712.

Photo courtesy of YWAM

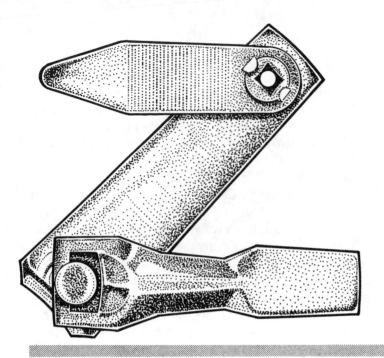

Zip Code

The Baptist Sunday School Board, one of the world's largest publishers of religious materials, spreads over several blocks in downtown Nashville, Tennessee, and employs some fifteen hundred people. It serves the Southern Baptist Convention, the world's largest Protestant denomination.

The board's postal budget alone is more than two million dollars annually, making Nashville second only to Washington, D.C., in the volume of second-class mail shipped.

The volume is so great that the Sunday School Board has its own zip code!

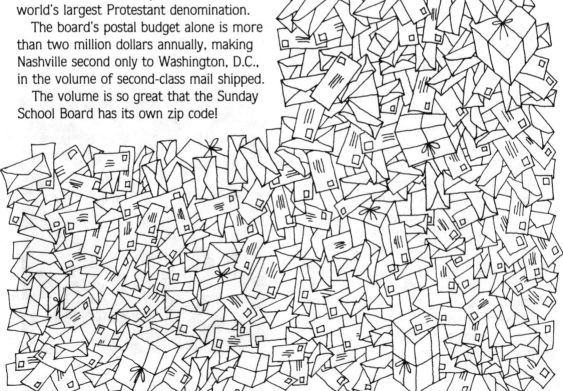

About the Author

Bob Flood has been interested in writing for as long as he can remember. In seventh grade, he even put out his own newspaper, called *The Porcupine Quills.* After attending Moody Bible Institute and then graduating from California Polytechnic State University, Bob's jobs have included that of editor (three years) and administrative director (six years) of *Moody Monthly,* and director of editorial and production (one year) at Moody Press. Currently Bob is a free-lance author and magazine consultant. His special interests in travel and American history show up, not only in this book, but also in several others of his: *America, God Shed His Grace on Thee; Men Who Shaped America;* and *The Christian's Vacation and Travel Guide.* Bob lives in Olympia Fields, Illinois, with his wife Lorelei and son David.

About the Artist

As a young boy, Britt Collins never planned on being an artist. But as his father took him to numerous museums and historic sites, Britt developed his ability to observe. Before graduating from Virginia Commonwealth University with a degree in art and design, Britt won second place in the nation with his illustration for the Dannon Yogurt poster competition, and was twice recognized by the Society of Illustrators. He then served as art director of *His Magazine,* and presently is a free-lance illustrator and designer, working on magazine and book covers for both Christian and secular publishers. Some of Britt's special interests appear in this book, including sports cars, tropical islands, World War II fighter planes, and Civil War history. Britt lives in Wheaton, Illinois, with his wife Patricia and infant son Taylor.

A Word to Parents and Teachers

I was browsing one day in a Chicago area bookstore and picked up *The Macmillan Illustrated Almanac for Kids.* The cover promised "fascinating facts, amazing stories, and important things you should know."

Inside it seemed to contain a little of everything—from science to celebrities, from history to the problems of adolescence.

The Christian scene, both past and present, also abounds with "fascinating facts, amazing stories, and important things you should know." Christian families and schools need a book of this kind, I concluded, with stories about God's people, and with content teaching truly Christian values.

So originated *The Christian Kids Almanac.* But it's not a book for kids only. This is a book to help educate parents and teachers, as well as young readers, about God's work in and through his people in modern times, and specifically in America.

I have tried to achieve a good balance between today's world and the America of yesterday. The average family, tragically, knows little about the details of this nation's rich Christian heritage. The public schools, of course, do not teach it. Some Christian schools do an admirable job in this area, but may not be able to keep up on events in present-day Christianity. And so many children never learn of America's spiritual history or of God's continuing work here today.

As God constantly reminded the children of Israel to remember all that he had done for them, so God wants this nation not to forget how he has moved on this continent, and still moves. If we neglect to educate the younger generation in this area, they may conclude that God acted among his people long ago in Israel, but does not act today!

How can you make the best use of this book?

You may want to incorporate an item or two in family or classroom devotions from time to time, to promote thought and discussion.

You can encourage children to use the book as a reference to supplement what they learn at public school or on tv about science, history, and even sports. In a Christian school, children can use this book's topical index to help them find appropriate material for reports.

Your whole family can use it as a resource guide to other Christian books, magazines, films, music camps, and youth movements.

But best of all, just leave it out on a table or counter or desk for leisure reading. Dip into it yourself from time to time. Like the popular books of lists, trivia books, and books of world records, *The Christian Kids Almanac* is laid out in bits and pieces. It's designed so that you can read an item now and another later. But I hope you'll find the content fascinating enough that, once you've begun reading, you'll just put on the "cruise control" and keep going!

Bob Flood
Olympia Fields, Illinois

Index

Answers to puzzles on pages 156-157:

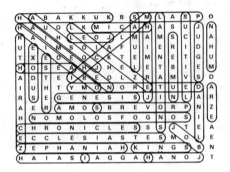

Answers to ham codes on page 88:

GM = good morning
GA = go ahead
QSY = change frequency
WX = weather
TVI = television interference
TU = thank you
TT = that
QTO = Have you left port?
XTAL = crystal
XMTR = transmitter